THE SINFULNESS AND CURE OF THOUGHTS

THE SINFULNESS AND CURE OF THOUGHTS

REV. STEPHEN CHARNOCK
FORMERLY FELLOW OF NEW COLLEGE, OXFORD

MINNEAPOLIS

Published by Curiosmith.
Minneapolis, Minnesota.
Internet: curiosmith.com.

Previously published as part of *A Supplement to the Morning-Exercise at Cripple-gate: or, Several more Cases of Conscience Practically Resolved by Sundry Ministers,* Samuel Annesley, edit., London: Thomas Cockerill, 1674.

The text for this edition is from: *The Morning Exercises at Cripplegate, St. Giles in the Fields and Southwark; etc.,* Vol. 2, James Nichols, edit., London: Thomas Tegg, 1844.

Unless otherwise stated, the notes and quotes in the footnotes are the original Greek and Latin notes translated into English by James Nichols (1785–1861). When a translation exists, Latin and Greek phrases are sometimes omitted for ease of reading.

The biography is from: Samuel Dunn. *Memoirs of the Seventy-Five Eminent Divines Whose Discourses Form the Morning Exercises at Cripplegate, St. Giles in the Fields, and in Southwark.* London: John Snow, 1844.

Elizabethan verbs and pronouns are updated to modern English word for word.

The "Guide to the Contents" was added to this edition by the publisher.

ISBN 9781946145567

GUIDE TO THE CONTENTS

Biographical Sketch of Rev. Stephen Charnock. (Page 9)

The words of the Genesis 6:5. (Page 17)

WHAT KIND OF THOUGHTS ARE SINS. (Page 21)

I. Negatively—A simple apprehension of sin is not sinful. (Page 21)

II. Positively—Our thoughts may be branched in two parts. (Page 23)
- 1. First motions. (Page 23)
- 2. Voluntary thoughts. (Page 24)

VOLUNTARY THOUGHTS. (Page 24)

I. In regard of God. (Page 24)
- 1. Cold thoughts of God. (Page 24)
- 2. Debasing conceptions unworthy of God. (Page 25)
- 3. Accusing thoughts of God. (Page 26)
- 4. Curious thoughts about things too high for us. (Page 26)

II. In regard of ourselves. (Page 27)
- 1. Ambitious thoughts. (Page 27)
- 2. Self-confident. (Page 27)
- 3. Self-applauding. (Page 28)
- 4. Ungrounded imaginations of the events of things. (Page 28)
- 5. Immoderate thoughts about lawful things. (Page 29)

III. In regard to others—Envious, censorious, jealous, and revengeful. (Page 29)

FURTHER GUILT IN OUR THOUGHTS. (Page 31)
- 1. Delight in them. (Page 31)
- 2. Contrivance: when the delight in the thought grows up to the contrivance of the act. (Page 33)
- 3. Re-acting sin after it is outwardly committed. (Page 34)

PROOF THAT THEY ARE SINS. (Page 36)
- 1. They are contrary to the law. (Page 36)
- 2. They are contrary to the order of our nature. (Page 38)
- 3. We are accountable to God. (Page 40)

THE PROVOCATION THERE IS IN THOUGHTS. (Page 43)

1. In respect of fruitfulness. (Page 44)
2. In respect of quantity. (Page 45)
3. In respect of strength. (Page 49)
4. In respect of alliance. (Page 50)
5. In respect of contrariety and odiousness to God. (Page 52)
6. In respect of connaturalness and voluntariness. (Page 53)

Uses.
Use 1—Reproof. (Page 56)
Use 2—Exhortation. (Page 58)

Directions. (Page 60)

I. Raising good thoughts. (Page 60)
1. Get renewed hearts. (Page 61)
2. Study Scripture. (Page 62)
3. Reflect often upon your first conversion. (Page 64)
4. Ballast your heart with a love to God. (Page 66)
5. Exercise faith. (Page 67)
6. Accustom yourself to a serious meditation every morning. (Page 69)
First—The matter of your meditation. (Page 70)
Secondly—The manner of your meditation. (Page 72)
7. Draw spiritual inferences from occasional objects. (Page 74)

II. Preventing bad thoughts. (Page 76)
1. Exercise frequent humiliations. (Page 76)
2. Avoid entangling yourselves with the world. (Page 77)
3. Avoid idleness. (Page 78)
4. Awe your hearts with the thoughts of God's omniscience, especially the discovery of it at the last judgment. (Page 79)
5. Keep a constant watch over your hearts. (Page 81)

III. Ordering evil thoughts when they do intrude. (Page 84)
1. Examine them. (Page 84)
2. Check them in the first appearance. (Page 85)
3. Improve them. (Page 87)
4. Continue your resistance. (Page 89)
5. Join supplication with your opposition. (Page 90)

IV. Concerning good thoughts. (Page 91)

GUIDE TO THE CONTENTS *(Continued)*

1. Welcome and entertain them. (PAGE 91)
2. Improve them for these ends to which they naturally tend. (PAGE 93)
3. Refer to them to assist your morning meditation. (PAGE 95)
4. Record the choicer of them. (PAGE 96)
5. Back them with ejaculations. (PAGE 97)

Biographical Sketch of

Rev. Stephen Charnock B.D.

This learned divine and excellent preacher was a descendant of a respectable family in Lancashire, and was born in London, in 1628, where his father practiced as a solicitor. He commenced his studies at Emmanuel College, Cambridge, under the tuition of Dr. Sancroft, and, while there, was made a new creature in Christ Jesus. On quitting the university, he exercised his ministry at Southwark, where he was made instrumental in the conversion of seven or eight persons. In 1649 he went to Oxford, and in the following year obtained a fellowship in New College. In 1652 he was incorporated A.M., as he had before stood in Cambridge. Two years after he became senior proctor of the university, "being then taken notice of," says Wood, "by the godly party for his singular gifts, and had in reputation by the then most learned Presbyterians; and therefore he was the more frequently put upon public work." In 1656 he went to Dublin, and resided in the family of Sir Harry Cromwell, lieutenant of Ireland. He exercised his ministry in that city with almost universal approbation. The Restoration putting an end to his ministry there, he returned to London, where he spent fifteen years in retirement, and, for his further improvement, took a tour occasionally to France and Holland. In 1675 he accepted a call to become joint-pastor of a congregation in Crosby-square, with the Rev. Thomas Watson, where he continued till removed by death, July 27, 1680, aged fifty-two. His remains were conveyed to his meeting-house in Crosby-square, and from thence to St. Michael's Church, Cornhill. His funeral sermon was preached by the Rev. John Johnson, his fellow-collegian. It is difficult to speak too highly of this great and good man. He was, as to manners and deportment, venerable and grave, like an aged person, from his youth; a man of excellent abilities, strong judgment, and singular genius. His attainments in learning were of the first order, having been throughout life a most diligent and methodical student, and a great redeemer of time, rescuing not only his restless hours in the night, but even the time that was spent in walking, from those impertinences which so often fill up the mind and steal away the heart from nobler objects. He constantly wrote down his thoughts upon those occasions, which furnished him with many materials for his most elaborate discourses. With the learned languages he had a very extensive acquaintance. Mr. Johnson said, "he never knew a man in all his life who had attained near to that skill that Mr. Charnock had in the originals of the Old and New Testament, except Mr. Thomas Cawton." In the talent of preaching he had few equals. His sermons were chiefly of a practical nature, yet rational and argumentative, reaching to the understandings as well as the affections of his hearers. When controversies came in his way he discussed them with great acuteness and judgment, and discovered no less skill in applying them to practice. Though his preaching was considered by some persons as too high for the vulgar, yet, if sometimes deep, he was never abstruse, and handled the great truths of the gospel with much clearness. In his younger days he delivered his sermons without notes, but as he grew in years he penned and read them *verbatim.* Though he was not popular, on account of his disadvantageous way of reading with a glass, yet his preaching was much esteemed by the more judicious sort of hearers. He spent most of his time in his study, which made him somewhat reserved in conversation; but where he was well acquainted, he could be very free and communicative; and he selected his society from the more serious as well as intelligent part of mankind. His library, furnished with a curious, though not a very large, collection of books, was unfortunately destroyed in the fire of London. In such reputation was he held by his brethren, that many able ministers loved to sit at his feet, for the benefit of those instructions which they could not get by many books, or by the sermons of others. In the course of his ministry at Crosby-square he intended to have delivered a complete body of divinity, but his sun was set at the threshold of this design. He had entered upon a set of discourses on the Existence and Attributes of God, which he did not live to finish. While he treated upon these subjects, they inspired him with so lively an interest in them as seemed to indicate his near and rapid approach to his everlasting rest. It was for some time before his death his longing desire to be in heaven, where there is the perfection of holiness; and he expressed a lively hope that he should quickly enjoy that felicity.

The sermon in the Morning Exercises, on The Sinfulness and Cure of Evil Thoughts, was the only thing published by Mr. Charnock. After his death, the Rev. R. Adams and the Rev. E. Veal, to whom he committed his papers, published his Discourse on Divine Providence, in 1680, and his Discourses on the Existence and Attributes of God, in 1681, in one large volume folio; to which was afterwards added another volume, consisting of discourses on Regeneration, Reconciliation, The Lord's Supper, and various other important subjects. His Two Discourses on Man's Enmity to God, and on the

Salvation of Sinners, were printed in 1699. The Rev. Augustus Toplady says, "I have met with many treatises on the Divine Perfections, but with none which any way equals that of Mr. Charnock. Perspicuity and depth, metaphysical sublimity and evangelical simplicity, immense learning and plain but irrefragable reasoning, conspire to render that performance one of the most inestimable productions that ever did honor to the sanctified judgment and genius of a human being. If I thought myself at all adequate to the task, I would endeavor to circulate the outlines of so rich a treasure into more hands, by reducing the substance of it within the compass of an octavo volume. Was such a design properly executed, a more important service could hardly be rendered to the cause of religion, virtue, and knowledge. Many people are frightened at a folio of more than 800 pages, who might have both leisure and inclination to avail themselves of a well-digested compendium."

The Sinfulness and Cure of Thoughts

by Rev. Stephen Charnock, B.D.

And God saw that the wickedness of man was great in the earth, and that every imagination of the thoughts of his heart was only evil continually. —Genesis 6:5.

I know not a more lively description in the whole book of God of the natural corruption derived from our first parents, than these words; wherein you have the ground of that grief, which lay so close to God's heart, (verse 6) and the resolve thereupon to destroy man, and whatsoever was serviceable to that ungrateful creature. That must be highly offensive which moved God to repent of a fabric so pleasing to him at the creation; every stone in the building being at the first laying pronounced "good" by him; and upon a review, at the finishing the whole, he left it the same character with an emphasis, "*very* good."[1] There was not a

1 Genesis 1:31.

pin in the whole frame but was very "beautiful;"[1] and being wrought by Infinite "Wisdom," it was "a very comely piece of art."[2,3] "What, then, should provoke him to repent of so excellent a work?" "The wickedness of man," which "was great in the earth." "How came it to pass that man's wickedness should swell so high? Whence did it spring?" From the "imagination." "Though these might be sinful imaginations, might not the superior faculty preserve itself untainted?" Alas! that was defiled; the "imagination of the thoughts was evil." "But though running thoughts might wheel-about in his mind, yet they might leave no stamp or impression upon the will and affections." Yes, they did: the "imagination of the thoughts of his heart was evil." "Surely all could not be under such a blemish: were there not now and then some pure flashes of the mind?" No, not one: "Every imagination." "But granting that they were evil, might there not be some fleeting good mixed with them, as a poisonous toad hath something useful?" No: "Only evil!" "Well, but there might be some intervals of thinking; and though there was no good thought, yet evil ones were not always rolling there." Yes, they were "continually;" not a moment of time that man was free from them. One would scarce imagine such an

1 Ecclesiastes 3:11.

2 Eusebii *Praepar. Evang.*

3 Psalm 104:24.

inward nest of wickedness; but God has affirmed it; and if any man should deny it, his own heart would give him the lie. Let us now consider the words by themselves:—

יֵצֶר "Imagination," properly signifies *figmentum*, of יָצַר "to afflict, press, or form a thing by way of compression." And thus it is a metaphor taken from a potter's framing a vessel, and extends to "whatsoever is framed" inwardly in the heart, or outwardly in the work. It is usually taken by the Jews for that fountain of sin within us. Mercer tells us, it is always used in an evil sense.[1] But there are two places, if no more, wherein it is taken in a good sense: Isaiah 26:3: יֵצֶר סָמוּךְ "Whose mind is stayed;" and 1 Chronicles 29:18, where David prays, that a disposition to offer willingly to the Lord might be preserved "in the imagination of the thoughts of the heart of the people." Indeed, for the most part it is taken for "the evil imaginations" of the heart, as Deuteronomy 31:21; Psalm 81:12, etc. The Jews make a double "figment," a good and bad; and fancy two angels assigned to man, one bad, another good; which Maimonides interprets to be nothing else but natural corruption and reason.[2] This word "imagination" being joined with "thoughts," implies not only the complete thoughts,

---

1 Mercerus *in loc.*

2 Maimonidis *More Nevochim*, pars iii. cap. 22. Amanæ *Censura, in loc.*

but the first motion or formation of them, to be evil.

The word "heart" is taken variously in Scripture. It signifies properly that inward member which is the seat of the vital spirits: but sometimes it signifies, 1. The *understanding and mind*—Psalm 12:2: "With a double heart do they speak;" that is, with a double mind. See also Proverbs 8:5. 2. For the *will.*—2 Kings 10:30: "All that is in my heart," that is, in my will and purpose. 3. For the *affections.*—As, Deuteronomy 6:5: "Thou shalt love the Lord thy God with all thine heart;" that is, with all thy affections. 4. For *conscience.*—2 Samuel 24:10: "David's heart smote him;" that is, his conscience checked him. But "heart" here is used for the whole soul, because—according to Pareus's note—the soul is chiefly seated in the heart, especially the will, and the affections, her attendants; because, when any affection stirs, the chief motion of it is felt in the heart. So that, by the "imaginations of the thoughts of the heart" are here meant all the inward operations of the soul, which play their part principally in the heart; whether they be the acts of the understanding, the resolutions of the will, or the blusterings of the affections.

Only evil—The Vulgar mentions not the exclusive particle רַק and so enervates the sense of the place. But our neighbor-translations either express it as we do, "only;" or to that sense, that they were "certainly," or, "no other than, evil."

Continually—The Hebrew, כָּל־הַיּוֹם "all the day," or, "every day." Some translations express it *verbatim* as the Hebrew. Not a moment of a man's life wherein our hereditary corruption does not belch-out its froth, even "from his youth," (as God expounds it, Genesis 8:21) to the end of his life.

Whether we shall refer the general wickedness of the heart in the text to that age, as some of the Jesuits do, because after the deluge God does not seem so severely to censure it;[1] or rather take the exposition [which] the learned Rivet gives of it, referring the first part of the verse ("And God saw that the wickedness of man was great in the earth") to those times; and the second part to the universal corruption of man's nature, and the root of all sin in the world;[2] the Jesuits' argument will not be very valid, for the extenuation of original corruption, from Genesis 8:21. For if man's imaginations be "evil from his youth," what is it but in another phrase to say they were so "continually?" But, suppose it be understood of the iniquity of that age, may it not be applied to all ages of the world? David complains of the wickedness of his own time, Psalm 14:3; 5:9; yet St. Paul applies it to all mankind, Romans 3:12, 13. Indeed it seems to be a description of man's natural depravity, by

1 Genesis 8:21.

2 Rivetus *in Gen. exercit.* 51.

God's words after the deluge, Genesis 8:21, which are the same in sense, to show that man's nature, after that destroying judgment, was no better than before. Every word is emphatical, exaggerating man's defilement: wherein consider the universality, 1. Of the *subject:* "Every man." 2. Of the *act:* "Every thought." 3. Of the *qualification of the act:* "Only evil." 4. Of the *time:* "Continually."

The words thus opened afford us this proposition:

"That the thoughts and inward operations of the souls of men are naturally, universally evil and highly provoking."

Some by "cogitation" mean not only the acts of the understanding, but those of the will, yea, and the sense too. But indeed that which we call "cogitation," or "thought," is the work of the mind; "imagination," of the fancy.[1] It is not properly thought, till it be wrought by the understanding; because the fancy was not a power designed for thinking, but only to receive the images impressed upon the sense, and concoct them, that they might be fit matter for thoughts; and so it is the exchequer, wherein all the acquisitions of sense are deposited, and from thence received by the intellective faculty. So that thoughts are *inchoativè* in the fancy, *consummativè* in the understanding, *terminativè* in all the other faculties. Thought first engenders opinion in the

1 Cartesii *Princip. Philos*. pars. i. sect. 9.

mind; thought spurs the will to consent or dissent; it is thought also which spirits the affections.

I will not spend time to acquaint you with the methods of their generation. Every man knows he has a thinking faculty, and some inward conceptions, which he calls "thoughts;" he knows that he thinks, and what he thinks; though he be not able to describe the manner of their formation in the womb, or remember it any more than the species of his own face in a glass.

In this discourse let us first see what kind of thoughts are sins.

I. Negatively. *A simple apprehension of sin is not sinful.*—Thoughts receive not a sinfulness barely from the object: *that* may be unlawful to be acted *which* is not unlawful to be thought-of. Though the will cannot will sin without guilt, yet the understanding may apprehend sin without guilt; for that does no more contract a pollution by the bare apprehension, than the eye does by the reception of the species of a loathsome object. Thoughts are morally evil, when they have a bad principle, want a due end, and converse with the object in a wrong manner. Angels cannot but understand the offense which displaced the apostate stars from heaven; but they know not sin *cognitione practicâ* ["with a practical cognizance"]. Glorified saints may consider their former sins, to enhance their admirations of pardoning mercy. Christ himself must needs understand the matter of the devil's temptation; yet Satan's suggestions to his thoughts were as the vapors of a jakes[1] mixed with the sun-beams, without a defilement of them. Yea, God himself, who is infinite purity, knows the object of his own acts, which are conversant about sin: as his holiness in forbidding it, wisdom in permitting, mercy in pardoning, and justice in punishing. But thoughts of sin in Christ, angels, and glorified saints, are accompanied with an abhorrency of it, without any combustible matter in them to be kindled by it. As our thoughts of a divine object are not gracious, unless we love and delight in it; so a bare apprehension of sin is not positively criminal, unless we delight in the object apprehended. As a sinful object does not render our thoughts evil, so a divine object does not render them good; because we may think of it with undue circumstances, as unseasonably, coldly, etc. And thus there is an imperfection in the best thought a regenerate man has; for though I will suppose he may have a sudden ejaculation without the mixture of any positive impurity, and a simple apprehension of sin with a detestation of it, yet there is a defect in each of them; because it is not with that raised affection to God, or intense abhorrency of sin, as is due from us to such objects, and whereof we were capable in our primitive state.

1 Jakes—a house of office or back-house; a privy. *(Webster's 1828 Dictionary.)*

II. Positively. Our thoughts may be branched into *first motions,* or *such that are more voluntary*—

1. *First motions.*—Those unfledged thoughts and single threads, before a multitude of them come to be twisted and woven into a discourse; such as skip-up from our natural corruption, and sink down again, as fish in a river. These are sins, though we consent not to them; because, though they are without our will, they are not against our nature; but spring from an inordinate frame, of a different hue from what God implanted in us. How can the first sprouts be good, if the root be evil? Not only the thought formed, but the very formation, or first imagination, is evil. Voluntariness is not necessary to the essence of a sin, though it be to the aggravation of it. It is not my will or knowledge which does make an act sinful, but God's prohibition. Lot's incest was not ushered by any deliberate consent of his will; yet who will deny it to be a sin? since he should have exercised a severer command over himself than to be overtaken with drunkenness, which was the occasion of it.[1] Original sin is not *effectivè* voluntary in infants, because no act of the will is exerted in an infant about it; yet it is voluntary *subjectivè,* because it does *inhoerere voluntati* ["inhere in the will"]. These motions may be said to be voluntary negatively, because the will does not set bounds to them, and exercise that

1 Genesis 19:33–35.

sovereign dominion over the operations of the soul which it ought to do, and wherewith it was at its first creation invested. Besides, though the will does not immediately consent to them, yet it consents to the occasions which administer such motions; and therefore, according to the rule that *causa causae est causa causati*,[1] may be justly charged upon our score.[2]

2. *Voluntary thoughts*.—Which are the blossoms of these motions; such that have no lawful object, no right end, not governed by reason, eccentric, disorderly in their motions, and like the jarring strings of an untuned instrument. The meanest of these floating fancies are sins, because we act not, in the production of them, as rational creatures; and what we do without reason, we do against the law of our creation, which appointed reason for our guide, and the understanding to be to το ἡγεμονικον, "the governing power" in our souls.

These may be reduced to three heads: I. *In regard of God*. II. *Of ourselves*. III. *Of others*.

I. *In regard of God*.

1. *Cold thoughts of God*.—When no affection is raised in us by them; when we delight not in God, the object of those thoughts, but in the

---

1 "The cause of a cause is also the cause of that which is subsequently caused." *(Nichols' trans.)*

2 This entire sentence was added by the author in the second edition.—NICHOLS.

thought itself, and operation of our mind about him, consisting of some quaint notion of God of our own conceiving; this is to delight in the act or manner of thinking, not in the object thought-of: and thus these thoughts have a folly and vanity in them. They are also sinful in a regenerate man, in respect of the faintness of the understanding, not acting with that vigor and sprightliness, nor with those raised and spiritual affections, which the worth of such an object does require.

2. *Debasing conceptions unworthy of God.*— Such are called in the Heathen "vain imaginations;"[1] διαλογισμοις, their "reasonings about" God; who as they glorified not God as God, so they did not think of God as God, according to the dignity of a Deity. Such a mental idolatry may be found in us, when we dress-up a God according to our own humors, humanize him, and ascribe to him what is grateful to us, though never so base: "Thou thoughtest that I was altogether such an one as thyself:"[2]—which is a grosser degrading of the Deity, than any representation of him by material images, because it is directly against his holiness, which is his glory, applauded chiefly by the angels, and an attribute which he swears by, as having the greatest regard to the honor of it.[3] Such an imagination Adam seemed

1 Romans 1:21.

2 Psalm 50:21.

3 Exodus 15:11; Isaiah 6:3; Psalm 89:35.

to have, conceiting God to be so mean a being that he, a creature not of a day's standing, could mount to an equality of knowledge with him.

3. *Accusing thoughts of God.*—Either of his mercy, as in despair; or of his justice, as too severe, as in Cain.[1] Of his providence: Adam conceited, yea, and charged God's providence to be an occasion of his crime: "The woman whom thou gavest to be with me."[2] His posterity are no juster to God, when they accuse him as a negligent governor of the world. "The Lord knoweth the thoughts of man, that they are vanity."[3] "What thoughts?" Injurious thoughts of his providence, as though God were ignorant of men's actions, or, at best, but an idle spectator of all the unrighteousness done in the world, not to "regard it," though he did "see" it.[4] And they in the prophet were of the same stamp, "that said in their heart, The Lord will not do good, neither will he do evil."[5] From such kind of thoughts most of the injuries from oppressors, and murmurings in the oppressed, do arise.

4. *Curious thoughts about things too high for us.*—It is the frequent business of men's minds to flutter about things without the bounds of

1 Genesis 4:13.

2 Genesis 3:12.

3 Psalm 94:11.

4 Psalm 94:7.

5 Zephaniah 1:12.

God's revelation. Not to be content with what God has published, is to accuse him, in the same manner as the serpent did to our first parents, of envying us an intellectual happiness: "God doth know that your eyes shall be opened."[1] Yet how do all Adam's posterity long after this forbidden fruit!

II. *In regard of ourselves.*—Our thoughts are proud, self-confident, self-applauding, foolish, covetous, anxious, unclean, and what not?

1. *Ambitious.*—The aspiring thought of the first man runs in the veins of his posterity. God took notice of such strains in the king of Babylon, when he said in his heart, "I will exalt my throne above the stars of God: I will ascend above the heights of the clouds; I will be like the Most High."[2] No less a charge will they stand under that settle themselves upon their own bottom, "establish their own righteousness," and will "not submit themselves unto the righteousness of God's" appointment.[3] The most forlorn beggar has sometimes thoughts vast enough to grasp an empire.

2. *Self-confident.*—Edom's thoughts swelled him into a vain confidence of a perpetual prosperity. "That saith in his heart, Who shall bring me down to the ground!"[4] And David sometimes said,

---

1 Genesis 3:5.

2 Isaiah 14:13, 14.

3 Romans 10:3.

4 Obadiah 1:3.

in the like state, that he should never be moved.

3. *Self-applauding.*—Either in the vain remembrances of our former prosperity, or ascribing our present happiness to the dexterity of our own wit. Such flaunting thoughts had Nebuchadnezzar at the consideration of his settling Babylon, the head and metropolis of so great an empire. "Is not this great Babylon, that I have built for the house of the kingdom?"[1] etc. Nothing more ordinary among men than over weening reflections upon their own parts, and thinking of themselves above what they ought to think.[2]

4. *Ungrounded imaginations of the events of things, either present or future.*—Such wild conceits, like meteors bred of a few vapors, do often frisk in our minds. (1.) *Of things present.*—It is likely Eve foolishly imagined she had brought-forth the Messiah, when she brought-forth a murderer. "I have gotten a man the Lord;"[3] as in the Hebrew, אִישׁ אֶת־יְהוָה believing, as some interpret, that she had brought-forth the promised seed. And such a brisk conceit Lamech seems to have had of Noah.[4] (2.) *Of things to come.*—Either in bespeaking false hopes, or antedating improbable griefs. Such are *the jolly thoughts* we have of a happy estate in

1 Daniel 4:30.

2 Romans 12:3.

3 Genesis 4:1.

4 Genesis 5:29.

reversion, which yet we may fall short of. Haman's heart leaped at the king's question, "What shall be done unto the man whom the king delighteth to honor?"[1] fancying himself the mark of his prince's favor, without thinking that a halter should soon choke his ambition. Or *perplexing thoughts* at the fear of some trouble, which is not yet fallen upon us, and perhaps never may. How did David torture his soul by his unbelieving fears, that he should "perish one day by the hand of Saul!"[2] These forestalling thoughts do really affect us: we often feel caperings in our spirits upon imaginary hopes, and shiverings upon conceited fears. These pleasing impostures, and self-afflicting suppositions, are signs either of an idle or indigent mind, that has no will to work, or only rotten materials to work upon.

5. *Immoderate thoughts about lawful things.*—When we exercise our minds too thick, and with a fierceness of affection above their merit; not in subserviency to God, or mixing our cares with dependencies on him. Worldly concerns may quarter in our thoughts; but they must not possess all the room, and thrust Christ into a manger; neither must they be of that value with us, as the law was with David, "sweeter than the honey or the honey-comb."

III. *In regard of others.*—All thoughts of our

1 Esther 6:6.

2 1 Samuel 27:1.

neighbor against the rule of charity. Such that "imagine evil in their hearts," God "hates."[1] These principally are, 1. *Envious.*—When we torment ourselves with others' fortunes. Such a thought in Cain, upon God's acceptance of his brother's sacrifice, was the prologue to, and foundation of, that cursed murder.[2] 2. *Censorious.*—Stigmatizing every freckle in our brother's conversation.[3] 3. *Jealous and evil surmises.*—Contrary to charity, which "thinketh no evil."[4] 4. *Revengeful.*—Such made Haman take little content in his preferments, as long as Mordecai refused to court him.[5] And Esau thought of "the days of mourning" for his father, that he might be revenged for his brother's deceits.[6]

There is no sin committed in the world, but is hatched in one or other of these thoughts. But, beside these, there are a multitude of other volatile conceits, like swarms of gnats, buzzing about us, and preying upon us, and as frequent in their successions as the curlings of the water upon a small breath of wind, one following another close at the heels. The mind is no more satisfied with thoughts than the first matter is with forms; continually shifting one for another, and many times the nobler

---

1 Zechariah 8:17.
2 Genesis 4:5.
3 1 Timothy 6:4.
4 1 Corinthians 13:5.
5 Esther 5:13.
6 Genesis 27:41.

for the baser; as when, upon the putrefaction of a human body, part of the matter is endued with the form of vermin. Such changeable things are our minds, in leaving that which is good for that which is worse, when they are inveigled by an active fancy and Bedlam affections. This "madness is in the heart of men while they live,"[1] and starts a thousand frenzies in a day. At the best, our fancy is like a carrier's bag, stuffed with a world of letters, having no dependence upon one another; some containing business, and others nothing but froth.

In all these thoughts there is a further guilt in three respects; namely, 1. *Delight;* 2. *Contrivance;* 3. *Re-acting.*

1. *Delight in them.*—The very tickling of our fancy by a sinful motion, though without a formal consent, is a sin, because it is a degree of complacency in an unlawful object; when the mind is pleased with the subject of the thought, as it has a tendency to some sensual pleasure, and not simply in the thought itself, as it may enrich the understanding with some degree of knowledge. The thought indeed of an evil thing may be without any delight in the evil of it. As philosophers delight in making experiments of poisonous creatures, without delighting in the poison as it is a noxious quality; we may delightfully think of sin without guilt, not delighting in it as sin, but as God, by his wise

1 Ecclesiastes 9:3.

providential ordering, extracts glory to himself, and good to his creature. In this case, though a sinful act be the material object of this pleasure, yet it is not the formal object; because the delight is not terminated in the sin, but in God's ordering the event of it to his own glory. But an inclination to a sinful motion, as it gratifies a corrupt affection, is sin; because every inclination is a malignant tincture upon the affections, including in its own nature an aversion from God, and testifying sin to be an agreeable object. And, without question, there can be no inclination to any thing, without some degree of pleasure in it; because it is impossible we can incline to that which we have a perfect abhorrency of. Hence it follows, that every inclination to a sinful motion is *consensus inchoatus*, or a "consent in embryo;" though the act may prove abortive. If we think of any unlawful thing with pleasure, and imagine it either in *fieri* or *facto esse,*[1] it brings a guilt upon us, as if it were really acted. As when upon the consideration of such a man's being my enemy, I fancy robbers rifling his goods, and cutting his throat, and rejoice in this revengeful thought, as if it were really done, it is a great sin; because it testifies an approbation of such a butchery, if any man had will and opportunity to commit it; and though it be a supposition, yet the

1 "Either as existing only in the fancy, or as an act previously performed." *(Nichols' trans.)*

act of the mind is really the same [as] it would be if the sinful act I think of were performed. Or, when a man conditionally thinks with himself, "I would steal such a man's goods, or kill such a person, if I could escape the punishment attending it," it is as if he did rob and murder him; because there is no impediment in his will to the commission of it, but only in the outward circumstances. Nay, though it be a mere *ens intentionale*, or *rationis*,[1] which is the object of the thought; yet the act of the mind is real, and as significant of the inclination of the soul, as if the object were real too: as, if a man has an unclean motion at the sight of a picture, which is only a composition of well-mixed and well-ordered colors, or at the appearance of the idea of a beauty framed in his own fancy; it is as much uncleanness as if it were terminated in some suitable object, the hinderance being not in the will, but in the insufficiency of the object to concur in such an act. Now, as the more delight there is in any holy service, the more precious it is in itself and more grateful to God; so, the more pleasure there is in any sinful motion, the more malignity there is in it.

2. *Contrivance.*—When the delight in the thought grows up to the contrivance of the act, which is still the work of the thinking faculty; when the mind does brood upon a sinful motion to hatch it up, and invents methods for performance, which

1 "A creature of the intention or of the reason." *(Nichols' trans.)*

the wise man calls "artificial inventions." חִשְּׁבֹנוֹת[1] So a learned man interprets διαλογισμοι πονηροι,[2] of "contrivances of murder, adultery," etc.[3] And the word signifies properly "reasonings;" when men's wits play the devils in their souls, in inventing sophistical reasons for the commission and justification of their crimes, with a mighty jollity at their own craft. Such plots are the trade of a wicked man's heart. A covetous man will be working in his inward shop from morning till night, to study new methods for gain: ("A heart exercised with covetous practices"[4]) and voluptuous and ambitious persons will draw schemes and models in their fancy of what they would outwardly accomplish: "They conceive mischief, and bring forth vanity, and their belly prepareth deceit."[5] Hence the thoughts are called "the counsels" and "devices of the heart;"[6] when the heart summons the head, and all the thoughts of it, to sit in debate, as a private junto, about a sinful motion.

3. *Re-acting sin after it is outwardly committed.*—Though the individual action be transient, and cannot be committed again; yet the idea and

1 Ecclesiastes 7:29.

2 Matthew 15:19.

3 Dr. Hammond on Matthew 15:19.

4 2 Peter 2:14.

5 Job 15:35.

6 1 Corinthians 4:5; Isaiah 32:7, 8.

image of it, remaining in the memory, may, by the help of an apish fancy, be repeated a thousand times over with a rarified pleasure: as both the features of our friends, and the agreeable conversations we have had with them, may with a fresh relish be represented in our fancies, though the persons were rotten many years ago.

Having thus declared the nature of our thoughts, and the degrees of their guilt, the next thing is, to prove that they are sins.

The Jews did not acknowledge them to be sins, unless they were blasphemous, and immediately against God himself.[1] Some Heathens were more orthodox, and among the rest Ovid, whose amorous pleasures, one would think, should have smothered such sentiments in him.[2] "The Lord," whose knowledge is infallible, "knoweth the thoughts of men, that they are vanity;"[3] yea, and of the wisest men, too, according to the apostle's interpretation.[4] And who were they that "became vain in their

---

1 Kimchi in Psalm 66, as quoted by Grotius in Matt. 5:20.

2 "Though thou may'st watch the body, yet the mind,
Against her will, can never be confined.
She will the adulteress act, spite of thy guard,
E'en though all entrance seems to be debarr'd:
For when the doors are closed with anxious care,
The heart is free, and hides the adulterer there."—Ovidii *Amorum*. lib. iii. Eleg. iv. 5. *(Nichols' trans.)*

3 Psalm 94:11.

4 1 Corinthians 3:20.

imaginations," but the wisest men the carnal world yielded?[1] the Grecians, the greatest philosophers; the Egyptians, their tutors; and the Romans, their apes. The elaborate operations of an unregenerate mind are fleshly.[2] If the whole web be so, needs must every thread. "The thought of foolishness is sin," that is, a foolish thought; not objectively a thought of folly, but one formally so; yea, "an abomination to the Lord."[3] As good thoughts and purposes are acts in God's account, so are bad ones. Abraham's intention to offer Isaac is accounted as an actual sacrifice: that the stroke was not given, was not from any reluctance of Abraham's will, but the gracious indulgence of God.[4] Sarah had a deriding thought; and God chargeth it as if it were an outward laughter and a scornful word.[5,6] Thoughts are the words of the mind, and as real in God's account as if they were expressed with the tongue.

There are three reasons for the proof of this, that they are sins:—

1. *They are contrary to the law.*—Which does forbid the first foamings and belchings of the heart; because they arise from an habitual corruption, and

1 Romans 1:21.

2 Romans 8:5–7.

3 Proverbs 24:9; 15:26.

4 Hebrews 11:17; James 2:21.

5 Genesis 18:12, 15.

6 "Therefore Sarah laughed within herself, saying," etc.—Targum. ["In her heart."]

testify a defect of something which the law requires to be in us, to correct the excursions of our minds. "I had not known lust, except the law had said, Thou shalt not covet."[1] Does not the law oblige man as a rational creature? Shall it then leave that part which does constitute him rational, to fleeting and giddy fancies? No; it binds the soul as the principal agent, the body only as the instrument. For if it were given only for the sensitive part, without any respect to the rational, it would concern brutes as well as men, which are as capable of a rational command and a voluntary obedience, as man without the conduct of a rational soul. It exacts a conformity of the whole man to God, and prohibits a difformity; and therefore engages chiefly the inward part, which is most the man. It must, then, extend to all the acts of the man; consequently to his thoughts, they being more the acts of the man than the motions of the body. Holiness is the prime excellency of the law, a title ascribed to it twice in one verse. "Wherefore the law is holy, and the commandment holy, and just, and good."[2] Could it be "holy," if it indulged looseness in the more noble part of the creature? Could it be "just," if it favored inward unrighteousness? Could it be "good," and useful to man, which did not enjoin a suitable conformity to God, wherein the creature's excellency lies? Can that

1 Romans 7:7.

2 Romans 7:12.

deserve the title of a *spiritual* law, that should only regulate the brutish part, and leave the spiritual to an unbounded licentiousness?[1] Can perfection be ascribed to that law, which does countenance the unsavory breathings of the spirit, and lay no stricter an obligation upon us than the laws of men?[2] Must not God's laws be as suitable to his sovereignty, as men's laws are to theirs? Must they not then be as extensive as God's dominion, and reach even to the privatest closets of the heart? It is not for the honor of God's holiness, righteousness, goodness, to let the spirit, which bears more flourishing characters of his image than the body, range wildly about without a legal curb.

2. *They are contrary to the order of nature, and the design of our creation.*—Whatsoever is a swerving from our primitive nature is sin, or at least a consequent of it. But all inclinations to sin are contrary to that righteousness wherewith man was first endued. "God hath made man upright; but they have sought out many inventions."[3] Man was created both with a disposition and ability for holy contemplations of God; the first glances of his soul were pure; he came every way complete out of the mint of his infinitely wise and good Creator; and when God pronounced all his creatures "good,"

---

1 Romans 7:14; James 1:25.

2 Matthew 5:28.

3 Ecclesiastes 7:29.

he pronounced man "very good" amongst the rest. But man is not now as God created him; he is off from his end; his understanding is filled with lightness and vanity. This disorder never proceeded from the God of order; Infinite Goodness could never produce such an evil frame; none of these loose "inventions" were of God's planting, but of man's seeking. No; God never created the intellective, no, nor the sensitive, part, to play Domitian's game, and sport itself in the catching of flies. "Man that is in honor, and understands not" that which he ought to understand, and thinks not that which he ought to think, "is like the beasts that perish."[1] He plays the beast, because he acts contrary to the nature of a rational and immortal soul. And such brutes we all naturally are, since the first woman believed her sense, her fancy, her affection, in their directions for the attainment of wisdom, without consulting God's law, or her own reason.[2] The fancy was bound by the right of nature to serve the understanding: it is then a slighting [of] God's wisdom to invert this order, in making *that* our governor *which* he made our subject. It is injustice to the dignity of our own souls to degrade the nobler part to a sordid slavery, in making the brute have dominion over the man; as if the horse were fittest to govern the rider. It is a falseness to God, and a

1 Psalm 49:20.

2 Genesis 3:6.

breach of trust, to let our minds be imposed upon by our fancy in giving it only feathers to dandle, and chaff to feed on, instead of those braver objects it was made to converse withal.

3. *We are accountable to God and punishable for thoughts.*—"If perhaps the thought of thine heart may be forgiven thee."[1] Nothing is the meritorious cause of God's wrath, but sin. The text tells us, that they were once the keys which opened the flood-gates of divine vengeance, and broached both the upper and nether cisterns to overflow the world. If they need a pardon, (as certainly they do) then if mercy does not pardon them, justice will condemn them. And it is absolutely said, that "a man of wicked devices," or "thoughts," God "will condemn."[2] אִישׁ מְזִמּוֹת "A man of thoughts," that is, "evil thoughts;" the word being usually taken in an ill sense. It is God's prerogative, often mentioned in Scripture, to "search the heart." To what purpose, if the acts of it did not fall under his censure, as well as his cognizance? He "weigheth the spirits,"[3] in the balance of his sanctuary and by the weights of his law, to sentence them, if they be found too light. The Word does discover, and judge them; it "divides asunder the soul and spirit," the sensitive part—the affections; and the rational—the

1 Acts 8:22.

2 Proverbs 12:2.

3 Proverbs 16:2.

understanding and will; both which it does dissect and open, and judge the acts of them, even "the thoughts and intents," ενθυμησεων και εννοιων, "whatsoever is within the θυμος, and whatsoever is within the νους," the one referring to "the soul," the other to "the spirit." These it passeth a judgment upon; as "a critic," κριτικος, censures the errata even to syllables and letters, in an old manuscript. These we are "to render an account of,"[1] as the Syriac renders those words, "With whom we have to do."[2] "Of what?" Of the first bubblings of the heart—"the notions and intents" of it. The least speck and atom of dust in every chink of this little world is known and censured by God. If our thoughts be not judged, God would not be a righteous Judge. He would not judge according to the merit of the cause, if outward actions were only scanned, without regarding the intents, wherein the principle and end of every action lies, which either swell or diminish the malignity of it. Actions, in kind the same, may have different circumstances in the thoughts, to heighten the one above the other; and if *they* were only judged, the most painted hypocrite might commence a blessed spirit at last, as well as the exactest saint. It is necessary also for the glory of God's omniscience. It is hereby chiefly that the extensiveness of God's knowledge is discovered,

1 Hebrews 4:12, 13.

2 Hebrews 4:13.

and that in order to "the praise" or dispraise of men; namely, to their justification or condemnation.[1] Those very thoughts will accuse thee before God's tribunal, which accuse thee here before conscience, his deputy. "Their thoughts the mean while"[2] (that is, in this life, while conscience bears witness) "accusing or else excusing one another; in the day when God shall judge the secrets of men;" that is—and also at the day of judgment, when conscience shall give-in its final testimony, upon God's examination of the secret counsels. This place is properly meant of those reasonings concerning good and evil in men's consciences, agreeable to the law of nature imprinted on them, which shall "excuse" them, if they practise accordingly, or "accuse" them, if they behave themselves contrary thereunto. But it will hold in this case; for if those inward approbations of the notions of good and evil will accuse us for our contrary practices, they will also accuse us for our contrary thoughts. Our good thoughts will be our accusers for not observing them, and our bad thoughts will be indictments against us for complying with them. It is probable, the soul may be bound-over to answer chiefly for these at the last day;[3] for the apostle charges Simon's guilt upon

1 1 Corinthians 4:5.

2 Romans 2:15, 16.

3 "Not only every evil work, but every thought of wickedness, will receive its due award of punishment."—HIERONYMUS *in Hos. vii. (Nichols' trans.)*

his "thought," not his word; and tells him, pardon must be principally granted for that.[1] The tongue was only an instrument to express what his heart did think, and would have been wholly innocent, had not his thoughts been first criminal. What, therefore, is the principal subject of pardon, would be so of punishment; as the first incendiaries in a rebellion are most severely dealt with. And if, as some think, the fallen angels were stripped of their primitive glory only for a conceived thought, how heinous must that be which has enrolled them in a remediless misery![2]

Having proved that there is a sinfulness in our thoughts, let us now see what provocation there is in them; which in some respects is greater than that of our actions. But we must take actions here *in sensu diviso*, as distinguished from the inward preparations to them. In the one, there is more of scandal; in the other, more of odiousness to God. God indeed does not punish thoughts so visibly, because, as he is Governor of the world, his judgments are shot against those sins that disturb human society; but he has secret and spiritual judgments for these, suitable to the nature of the sins.

Now thoughts are greater,

1 Acts 8:22.

2 This last sentence is not found in the first edition; between which and the second many other variations occur, much in favor of the latter.—NICHOLS.

1. *In respect of fruitfulness.*—"The wickedness" that "God saw great in the earth" was the fruit of "imaginations." They are the immediate causes of all sin. No cockatrice but was first an egg. It was a thought to be "as God," that was the first breeder of all that sin under which the world groans at this day; for Eve's mind was first "beguiled" in the alteration of her thought.[1] Since that, the lake of inward malignity acts all its evil by these smoking steams. "Evil thoughts" lead the van in our Saviour's catalogue,[2] as that which spirits all the black regiment which march behind. As good motions, cherished, will spring-up in good actions; so loose thoughts, favored, will break-out in visible plague-sores, and put fire unto all that wickedness which lies' habitually in the heart, as a spark may to a whole stock of gunpowder. The "vain babblings" of the soul, as well as those of the tongue, "will increase unto more ungodliness."[3] Being thus the cause, they include virtually in them all that is in the effect; as a seed contains in its little body the leaves, fruit, color, scent, which afterward appear in the plant. The seed includes all; but the color does not virtually include the scent, or the scent the color, or the leaves the fruit: so it is here, one act does not include the formal obliquity of another;

1 Genesis 3:5; 2 Corinthians 11:3.

2 Matthew 15:19.

3 2 Timothy 2:16.

but the thought which causes it does seminally include both the formal and final obliquity of every action; both that which is in the nature of it, and in the end to which it tends. As, when a tradesman cherishes immoderate thoughts of gain, and, in the attaining [of] it, runs "into many foolish and hurtful lusts;"[1] there is cheating, lying, swearing, to put-off the commodity; all these several acts have a particular sinfulness in the nature of the acts themselves, beside the tendency they have to the satisfying an inordinate affection; all which are the spawn of those first immoderate thoughts stirring-up greedy desires.

2. *In respect of quantity.*—"Imaginations" are said to be "continually evil." There is an infinite variety of conceptions—as the Psalmist speaks of the sea: "Wherein are things creeping innumerable, both small and great;"[2] and a constant generation of whole shoals of them—that you may as well number the fish in the sea, or the atoms in the sunbeams, as recount them.

There is a greater number in regard of the *acts,* and in regard of the *objects.*

1. *In regard of the acts of the mind:*—

(1.) *Antecedent acts.*—How many preparatory motions of the mind are there to one wicked external act! Yea, how many sinful thoughts are twisted

---

1 1 Timothy 6:9.

2 Psalm 104:25.

together to produce one deliberate sinful word! All which have a distinct guilt, and, if weighed together, would outweigh the guilt of the action abstractedly considered. How many repeated complacencies in the first motion, degrees of consent, resolved broodings, secret plottings, proposals of various methods, smothering contrary checks, vehement longings, delightful hopes, and forestalled pleasures, in the design![1] all which are but thoughts assenting or dissenting in order to the act intended. Upon a dissection of all these secret motions by the critical power of the word, we should find a more monstrous guilt than would be apparent in the single action for whose sake all these spirits were raised. There may be no sin in a material act, considered in itself, when there is a provoking guilt in the mental motion. A hypocrite's religious services are materially good, but poisoned by the imagination skulking in the heart, that gave birth unto them. It is "the wicked mind" or "thought" [that] makes the "sacrifice" (a commanding duty) "much more an abomination" to the Lord.[2]

(2.) *Consequent acts.*—When a man's fancy is pregnant with the delightful remembrance of the sin that is past, he draws-down a fresh guilt upon

1 "Wert thou, O man, to unlock the door of thy heart, thou wouldest find it to be a checkered storehouse and treasury of ills, and the seat of numberless passions."—PLUTARCHI *Moralia*, p. 500, *mihi*. *(Nichols' trans.)*

2 Proverbs 21:27. "With a wicked thought."

himself, (as they did in the prophet, "Yet she multiplied her whoredoms, in calling to remembrance the days of her youth,"[1] etc. "the lewdness of thy youth"[2]) in reviving the concurrence of the will to the act committed, making the sensual pleasure to commence spiritual, and, if ever there were an aching heart for it, revoking his former grief by a renewed approbation of his darling lust. Thus the sin of thoughts is greater in regard of duration. A man has neither strength nor opportunity always to act; but he may always think, and imagination can supply the place of action. Or if the mind be tired with sucking one object, it can, with the bee, presently fasten upon another. Senses are weary, till they have a new recruit of spirits; as the poor horse may sink under his burden, when the rider is as violent as ever. Thus old men may change their outward profaneness into mental wickedness; and as the Psalmist remembered his old songs,[3] so they their calcined sins in the night, with an equal pleasure. So that, you see, there may be a thousand thoughts as ushers and lackeys to one act, as numerous as the sparks of a new-lighted fire.

2. *In regard of the objects [which] the mind is conversant about.*—Such thoughts there are, and attended with a heavy guilt, which cannot probably,

---

1 Ezekiel 23:3, 19.

2 Ezekiel 23:21.

3 Psalm 77:5, 6.

no, nor possibly, descend into outward acts. A man may, in a complacent thought, commit fornication with a woman in Spain; in a covetous thought, rob another in the Indies; and in a revengeful thought, stab a third in America; and that while he is in this congregation. An unclean person may commit a mental folly with every beauty he meets. A covetous man cannot plunder a whole kingdom, but in one twinkling of a thought he may wish himself the possessor of all the estates in it. A Timon, a μισανθρωπος, ["misanthrope,"] cannot cut the throats of all the world; but, like Nero, with one glance of his heart he may chop-off the heads of all mankind at a blow. Ambitious men's practices are confined to a small spot of land; but with a cast of his mind he may grasp an empire as large as the four monarchies. A beggar cannot ascend a throne; but in his thoughts he may pass the guards, murder his prince, and usurp the government. Nay, further: an atheist may think "there is no God,"[1] that is, as some interpret it, wish there were no God, and thus in thought undeify God himself; though he may sooner dash heaven and earth in pieces than accomplish it. The body is confined to one object, and *that* narrow and proportionable to its nature; but the mind can wing itself to various objects in all parts of the earth. Where it finds none, it can make one; for fancy can compact several objects together,

1 Psalm 14:1.

coin an image, color a picture, and commit folly with it, when it has done; it can nestle itself in cobwebs spun out of its own bowels.

3. *In respect of strength.*—Imaginations of the heart are "only," that is, purely, "evil." The nearer any thing is in union with the root, the more radical strength it has. The first ebullitions of light and heat from the sun are more vigorous than the remoter beams; and the steams of a dunghill more noisome next that putrified body, than when they are dilated in the air. Grace is stronger in the heart-operations than in the outward streams; and sin more foul in the imagination of the thoughts of the heart, than in the act. In the text, the outward wickedness of the world is passed-over with a short expression; but the Holy Ghost dwells upon the description of the wicked "imagination," because *there* lay the mass. Man's "inward part is very wickednesses," קִרְבָּם הַוּוֹת[1] a whole nest of vipers. Thoughts are the immediate spawn of the original corruption, and therefore partake more of the strength and nature of it. Acts are more distant, being the children of our thoughts, but the grandchildren of our natural depravity. Besides, they lie nearest to that wickedness in the inward part, sucking the breast of that poisonous dam that bred them. The strength of our thoughts is also reinforced by being kept-in, for want of opportunity to act them; as liquors in

1 Psalm 5:9.

close glasses ferment and increase their sprightliness. "Musing," either carnal or spiritual, makes "the fire burn" the hotter;[1] as the fury of fire is doubled by being pent in a furnace. Outward acts are but the sprouts; the sap and juice lie in the wicked imagination or contrivance, which has a strength in it to produce a thousand fruits as poisonous as the former. "The members" are the "instruments," or "weapons," ὅπλα, "of unrighteousness:"[2] now, the whole strength which does manage the weapon lies in the arm that wields it; the weapon of itself could do no hurt without a force impressed. Let me add this too, that sin in thoughts is more simply sin. In acts there may be some occasional good to others; for a good man will make use of the sight of sin committed by others to increase his hatred of it; but in our sinful thoughts there is no occasion of good to others, they lying locked-up from the view of man.

4. *In respect of alliance.*—In these we have the nearest communion with the devil. The understanding of man is so tainted, that his "wisdom," the chiefest flower in it, is not only "earthly" and "sensual," (it were well if it were no worse!) but "devilish" too.[3] If the flower be so rank, what are the weeds? Satan's "devices" and our "thoughts" are of the same nature, and sometimes in Scripture expressed by the

1 Psalm 39:3.

2 Romans 6:13.

3 James 3:15.

same word, νοηματα.[1] As he has his devices, so have we, against the authority of God's law, the power of the gospel, and the kingdom of Christ. The devils are called "spiritual wickednesses,"[2] because they are not capable of carnal sins. Profaneness is an uniformity with the world, and intellectual sins are an uniformity with the god of it.[3] In verse 3 there is a double walking, answerable to a double pattern in verse 2: "Fulfilling the desires of the flesh" is a walking "according to the course of this world," or making the world our copy; and fulfilling the desires of the mind is a walking "according to the prince of the power of the air," or a making the devil our pattern. In carnal sins Satan is a tempter, in mental an actor. Therefore, in the one, we are conformed to his will; in the other, we are transformed into his likeness. In outward, we evidence more of obedience to his laws; in inward, more of affection to his person, as all imitations of others are. Therefore there is more of enmity to God, because more of similitude and love to the devil; a nearer approach to the diabolical nature implying a greater distance from the divine. Christ never gave so black a character as that of "the devil's children" to the profane world, but to the Pharisees, who had left the sins of men, to take-up those of devils, and were most guilty of those "high

1 2 Corinthians 2:11; 10:5.

2 Ephesians 6:12.

3 Ephesians 2:2, 3.

imaginations" which ought to be brought "into captivity to the obedience of Christ."

5. *In respect of contrariety and odiousness to God.*—"Imaginations" were "only evil;" and so most directly contrary to God, who is only good. Our natural "enmity against God" is seated in "the mind."[1] The sensitive part aims at its own gratification, and in men's serving their lusts they serve their pleasures: ("Serving divers lusts and pleasures")[2] but the το ἡγεμονικον, "the prince" in man is possessed with principles of a more direct contrariety; whence it must follow, that all the thoughts and counsels of it are tinctured with this hatred. They are, indeed, a defilement of the higher part of the soul, and that which belongs more peculiarly to God; and the nearer any part does approach to God, the more abominable is a spot upon it; as to cast dirt upon a prince's house, is not so heinous as to deface his image. The understanding, the seat of thoughts, is more excellent than the will; both because we know and judge before we will, and we will, or ought to will, only so much as the understanding thinks fit to be willed; and because God has bestowed the highest gifts upon it, adorning it with more lively lineaments of his own image. "Renewed in knowledge after the image of him that created him;"[3] implying

1 Romans 8:7.

2 Titus 3:3.

3 Colossians 3:10.

that there was more of the image of God at the first creation bestowed upon the understanding, the seat of knowledge, than on any other part, yea, than on all the bodies of men distilled together. "Father of spirits" is one of God's titles:[1] to bespatter his children, then, so near a relation, the jewel that he is choice of, must needs be more heinous. He being "the Father of spirits," this "spiritual wickedness" of nourishing evil thoughts is a cashiering all child-like likeness to him. The traitorous acts of the mind are most offensive to God; as it is a greater despite for a son to whom the father has given the greater portion, to shut him out of his house, only to revel in it with a company of roisters and strumpets, than in a child who never was so much the subject of his father's favor. And it is more heinous and odious, if these thoughts which possess our souls be at any time conversant about some idea of our own framing. It were not altogether so bad, if we loved something of God's creating, which had a physical goodness and a real usefulness in it to allure us; but to run wildly to embrace an *ens rationis*, to prefer "a thing of" no existence but what is colored by our own "imagination," of no virtue, no usefulness, a thing that God never created nor pronounced good—is a greater enmity and a higher slight of God.

6. *In respect of connaturalness and voluntariness.*—They are "the imaginations of the thoughts

1 Hebrews 12:9.

of the heart," and they are "continually evil." They are as natural as the aestuations of the sea, the bubblings of a fountain,[1] or the twinklings of the stars. The more natural any motion is, ordinarily the quicker it is. Time is requisite to action; but "thoughts have an instantaneous motion." The body is a heavy piece of clay; but "the mind can start-out on every occasion."[2] Actions have their stated times and places; but *these* solicit us and are entertained by us at all seasons. Neither day nor night, street nor closet, exchange nor temple, can privilege us from them: we meet them at every turn, and they strike upon our souls as often as light upon our eyes. There is no restraint for them: the laws of men, the constitution of the body, the interest of profit or credit, are mighty bars in the way of outward profaneness; but nothing lays the reins upon thoughts, but "the law of God;" and *this* man "is not subject to, neither can be."[3] Besides, the natural atheism in man is a special friend and nurse of these, few firmly believing either the omniscience of God, or his government of the world; which the Scripture speaks of frequently, as the cause of most sins among the sons of men.[4] Actions are done with some reluctance, and

---

1 "The indigenous fountains of evil."—PLUTARCHI *Moralia. (Nichols' trans.)*

2 THALES, in his Life by DIOGENES LAERTIUS.

3 Romans 8:7.

4 Isaiah 29:15; Ezekiel 9:9; Job 22:13, 14.

nips of natural conscience. Conscience will start at a gross temptation; but it is not frighted at thoughts. Men may commit speculative folly, and their conscience look on, without so much as a nod against it: men may tear out their neighbors' bowels in secret wishes, and their conscience never interpose to part the fray. Conscience, indeed, cannot take notice of all of them; they are too subtile in their nature, and too quick for the observation of a finite principle. They are many: "There are many devices in a man's heart,"[1] and they are nimble too; like the bubblings of a boiling pot, or the rising of a wave, that presently slides into its level; and, as Florus says of the Ligurians, "the difficulty is more to find, than conquer, them."[2] They are secret sins, and are no more discerned than motes in the air, without a spiritual sun-beam; whence David cries out, "Cleanse thou me from secret sins;"[3] which some explain of sins of thoughts, that were like sudden and frequent flashes of lightning, too quick for his notice, and unknown to himself. There is also more delight in them. There is less of temptation in them, and so more of election; and consequently more of the heart and pleasure in them, when they lodge with us. Acts of sin are troublesome; there is danger as well as pleasure in many of them: but there is no outward danger in

1 Proverbs 19:21.

2 Florus, lib. ii cap. 3.

3 Psalm 19:12.

thoughts; therefore the complacency is more compact and free from distraction. The delight is more unmixed, too, as intellectual pleasures are more refined than sensual. All these considerations will enhance the guilt of these inward operations.

USES

The uses shall be two, though many inferences might be drawn from the point.

USE I—REPROOF

What a mass of vanity should we find in our minds, if we could bring our thoughts in the space of one day, yea, but one hour, to an account! How many foolish thoughts with our wisdom, ignorant with our knowledge, worldly with our heavenliness, hypocritical with our religion, and proud with our humiliations! Our hearts would be like a grot, furnished with monstrous and ridiculous pictures; or as the wall in Ezekiel's vision, "portrayed" with "every form of creeping things, and abominable beasts;" a greater abomination than "the image of jealousy at the outward gate of the altar."[1] Were our inwards opened, how should we stand gazing both with scorn and wonder at our being such a pack of fools! Well may we cry out, with Agur, "We have not the understandings of men:"[2] we make not the use of

1 Ezekiel 8:5, 10.

2 Proverbs 30:2.

them, as is requisite for rational creatures; because we degrade them to attendances on a brutish fancy. I make no question, but were we able to know the fancies of some irrational creatures, we should find them more noble, heroic, and generous, *in suo genere*, than the thoughts of most men; more agreeable to their natures, and suited to the law of their creation. How little is God in any of our thoughts, according to his excellency! "God is not in all his thoughts."[1] No; our shops, our rents, our backs, and bellies usurp God's room. If any thoughts of God do start-up in us, how many covetous, ambitious, wanton, revengeful thoughts are jumbled together with them! Is it not a monstrous absurdity to place our friend with a crew of vipers, to lodge a king in a sty, and entertain him with the fumes of a jakes and dunghill? "The tongue of the just is as choice silver; the heart of the wicked is little worth;"[2] all the peddling wares and works in his inward shop are not valuable[3] with one silver drop from a gracious man's lips. It was an invincible argument of the primitive Christians for the purity of the Christian religion above all others in the world, that it did prohibit evil thoughts:[4] and is it not as unanswerable an argument

1 Psalm 10:4.

2 Proverbs 10:20.

3 "Not to be estimated in worth."—Nichols.

4 "Among us, even vain thoughts are considered to be culpable and sinful."—Minucius Felix. *(Nichols' trans.)*

that we are no Christians, if we give liberty to them? What is our moral conversation outwardly, but only a bare abstinence from sin—not a disaffection? Were we really and altogether Christians, would not that which is the chiefest purity of Christianity be our pleasure? and would we any more wrong God in our secret hearts than in the open streets? Is not thought a beam of the mind? and shall it be enamoured only on a dunghill? Is not the understanding the eye of the soul? and shall it behold only gilded nothings? It is "the flower of the spirit:"[1] shall we let every caterpillar suck it? It is the queen in us: shall every ruffian deflower it? It is as the sun in our heaven: and shall we besmear it with misty fancies? It was created, surely, for better purposes than to catch a thousand weight of spiders, as Heliogabalus employed his servants.[2] It was not intended to be made the common sewer of filthiness, or ranked among those ζωα ϖαμφαγα, ["gluttonous animals"] which eat not only fruit and flesh, but flies, worms, dung, and all sorts of loathsome materials.[3] Let not, therefore, our minds wallow in a sink of fantastical follies, whereby to rob God of his due, and our souls of their happiness.

USE II—EXHORTATION

We must take care for the suppression of them.

---

1 Plato.

2 Lampridius.

3 Aristotelis *Histor. Animal.* lib. viii.

All vice does arise from imagination.[1] Upon what stock does ambition and revenge grow, but upon a false conceit of the nature of honor? What engenders covetousness, but a mistaken fancy of the excellency of wealth? "Thoughts" must be forsaken, as well as our "way;" we cannot else have an evidence of a true conversion: ("Let the wicked forsake his way, and the unrighteous man his thoughts,"[2] etc.) and if we do not discard them, we are not likely to have an "abundant pardon;" and what will the issue of that be, but an abundant punishment? Mortification must extend to these: "affections" must be "crucified,"[3] and all the little brats of thoughts which beget them or are be gotten by them. Shall we nourish that which brought down the wrath of God upon the old world, as though there had not been already sufficient experiments of the mischief they have done? Is it not our highest excellency to be conformed to God in holiness, in as full a measure as our finite natures are capable? And is not God holy in his counsels and inward operations, as well as in his works? Has God any thoughts but what are righteous and just? Therefore, the more foolish and vain our imaginations are, the more are we "alienated from the life of God." The Gentiles were so, because they "walked in the vanity of their

1 Mirandula *De Imaginations*, cap. vii.

2 Isaiah 55:7.

3 Galatians 5:24.

mind;"[1] and we shall be so, if vanity walk and dwell in ours. As the tenth commandment forbids all unlawful thoughts and desires, so it obliges us to all thoughts and desires that may make us agreeable to the divine will, and like to God himself. We shall find great advantage by suppressing them: we can more easily resist temptations without, if we conquer motions within. Thoughts are the mutineers in the soul, which set open the gates for Satan; he has held a secret intelligence with them (so far as he knows them) ever since the fall; and they are his spies, to assist him in the execution of his devices. They prepare the tinder, and the next fiery dart sets all on a flame. Can we cherish these, if we consider that Christ died for them? He shed his blood for that which put the world out of order; which was accomplished by the sinful imagination of the first man, and continued by those imaginations mentioned in the text. He died to restore God to his right, and man to his happiness: neither of which can be perfectly attained, till those be thrown out of the possession of the heart.

That we may do this, let us consider these following directions; which may be branched into these heads: 1. *For the raising [of] good thoughts.* 2. *Preventing bad.* 3. *Ordering bad, when they do intrude.* 4. *Ordering good, when they appear in us.*

I. *For raising good thoughts.*

1 Ephesians 4:17, 18.

1. *Get renewed hearts.*—The fountain must be cleansed which breeds the vermin. Pure vapors can never ascend from a filthy quagmire. What issue can there be of a vain heart, but vain imaginations? Thoughts will not "become new," till a "man is in Christ."[1] We must be holy, before we can think holily. Sanctification is necessary for the dislodging of vain thoughts, and the introducing of good. "Wash thy heart from wickedness, that thou mayest be saved. How long shall thy vain thoughts lodge within thee?"[2] A sanctified reason would both discover and shame our natural follies. As all animal operations, so all the spiritual motions of our heads, depend upon the life of our hearts, as the *principium originis* ["the originating principle"].[3] As there is a "law in our members to bring us into captivity to the law of sin,"[4] so there must be a law in our minds to "bring our thoughts into captivity to the obedience of Christ."[5] We must "be renewed in the spirit of our minds,"[6] in our reasonings and thoughts, which are the "spirits" whereby the understanding acts, as the animal spirits are the instruments of corporeal motion. Till the understanding be born of the Spirit, it will delight in, and think of, nothing but

1 2 Corinthians 5:17.
2 Jeremiah 4:14.
3 Proverbs 4:23.
4 Romans 7:23.
5 2 Corinthians 10:5.
6 Ephesians 4:23.

things suitable to its fleshly original: but when it is spiritual, it receives new impressions, new reasonings and motions, suitable to the Holy Ghost, of whom it is born. "That which is born of the flesh is flesh; and that which is born of the Spirit is spirit."[1] A stone, if thrown upward a thousand times, will fall backward, because it is a forced motion; but if the nature of this stone were changed into that of fire, it would mount as naturally upward as before it sank downward. You may force some thoughts toward heaven sometimes; but they will not be natural, till nature be changed. Grace only gives stability, and prevents fluctuation, by fixing the soul upon God, as its chief end: "It is a good thing that the heart be established with grace:"[2] and what is our end will not only be first in our intentions, but most frequent in our considerations. Hence a sanctified heart is called in Scripture "a steadfast heart." There must be an enmity against Satan put into our hearts, according to the first promise, before we can have an enmity against his imps, or any thing that is like him.

2. *Study Scripture.*—Original corruption stuffs us with bad thoughts, and Scripture-knowledge would stock us with good ones; for it proposes things in such terms as exceedingly suit our imaginative faculty, as well as strengthen our understanding.

1 John 3:6.

2 Hebrews 13:9.

Judicious knowledge would make us "approve things that are excellent;"[1] and where such things are approved, toys cannot be welcome. Fullness is the cause of steadfastness: the cause of an intent and piercing eye is the multitude of animal spirits. Without this skill in the Word we shall have as foolish conceits of divine things, as ignorant men without the rules of art have of the sun and stars, or things in other countries which they never saw. The Word is called "a lamp to our feet," that is, the affections; "a light to our eyes," that is, the understanding.[2] It will direct the glances of our minds, and the motions of our affections. It "enlightens the eyes," and makes us have a new prospect of things; as a scholar, [who has] newly entered into logic, and studied the predicaments, etc., looks upon every thing with a new eye and more rational thoughts, and is mightily delighted with every thing he sees, because he eyes them as clothed with those notions he has newly studied. The devil had not his engines so ready to assault Christ, as Christ from his knowledge had Scripture-precepts to oppose him. As our Saviour by this means stifled thoughts offered, so by the same we may be able to smother thoughts arising in us. Converse therefore often with the Scripture, transcribe it in your heart, and turn it in *succum et sanguinem*, ["into nutritious moisture

1 Philippians 1:9, 10.

2 Psalm 119:105; 19:8.

and blood"] whereby a vigor will be derived into every part of your soul, as there is, by what you eat, to every member of your body. Thus you will make your mind Christ's library, as Jerome speaks of Nepotianus.[1]

3. *Reflect often upon the frame of your mind at your first conversion.*—None have more settled and more pleasant thoughts of divine things than new converts, when they first clasp about Christ; partly because of the novelty of their state, and partly because God puts a full stock into them; and diligent tradesmen at their first setting-up have their minds intent upon improving their stock. Endeavor to put your mind in the same posture [in which] it was then. Or if you cannot tell the time when you did first close with Christ, recollect those seasons wherein you have found your affections most fervent, your thoughts most united, and your mind most elevated; as when you renewed repentance upon any fall, or had some notable cheerings from God; and consider what matter it was which carried your heart upward, what employment you were engaged in, when good thoughts did fill your soul; and try the same experiment again. Asaph would oppose God's ancient works to his murmuring thoughts: he would remember his "song

---

1 "By assiduous reading and continued meditation, he had made his breast the library of Christ."—HIERONYMI *Epist.* iii. *(Nichols' trans.)*

in the night," that is, the matter of his song, and read over the records of God's kindness.[1] David too would "never forget," that is, frequently renew the remembrance of, those precepts whereby God had particularly quickened him.[2] Yea, he would reflect upon the places, too, where he had formerly conversed with God, to rescue himself from dejecting thoughts: "Therefore will I remember thee from the land of Jordan, and of the Hermonites, from the hill Mizar."[3] Some elevations surely David had felt in those places, the remembrance whereof would sweeten the sharpness of his present grief. When our former sins visit our minds, pleading to be speculatively re-acted, let us remember the holy dispositions we had in our repentance for them, and the thankful frames when God pardoned them. The disciples, at Christ's second appearance, reflected upon their own warm temper at his first discourse with them in a disguise, to confirm their faith, and expel their unbelieving conceits: "Did not our heart burn within us while he talked with us by the way, and while he opened to us the Scriptures?"[4] Strive to recollect truths, precepts, promises, with the same affection which possessed your souls when they first appeared in their glory and sweetness to you.

1 Psalm 77:6–12.

2 Psalm 119:93.

3 Psalm 42:6.

4 Luke 24:32.

4. *Ballast your heart with a love to God.*—David thought "all the day" of God's law, as other men do of their lusts, because he unexpressibly loved it: "O how love I thy law! it is my meditation all the day."[1] This was the successful means he used to stifle vain thoughts, and excite his hatred of them: "I hate vain thoughts; but thy law do I love."[2] It is the property of love to think no evil:[3] it thinks good and delightful thoughts of God, friendly and useful thoughts of others. It fixes the image of our beloved object in our minds, [so] that it is not in the power of other fancies to displace it.[4] The beauty of an object will fasten a rolling eye: it is difficult to divorce our hearts and thoughts from that which appears lovely and glorious in our minds, whether it be God or the world. Love will, by a pleasing violence,[5] bind-down our thoughts, and hunt-away other affections: if it does not establish our minds, they will be like a cork, which, with a light breath, and a short curl of water, shall be tossed up and down from its station. Scholars that love learning will be continually hammering upon some notion or other which

1 Psalm 119:97.

2 Psalm 119:113.

3 1 Corinthians 13:5.

4 "Æneas is my thoughts' perpetual theme,
Their daily longing, and their nightly dream."—Ovidii *Heroid.* ep. vii. 25. *(Dryden's trans.)*

5 "Love is a certain violent affection."—Luciani *Dialogi.* *(Nichols' trans.)*

may further their progress, and as greedily clasp it as the iron will its beloved loadstone. He that is "winged with a divine love" to Christ will have frequent glances and flights toward him,[1] and will start-out from his worldly business several times in a day to give him a visit. Love, in the very working, is a settling grace; it increases our delight in God, partly by the sight of his amiableness, which is cleared to us in the very act of loving, and partly by the recompenses he gives to the affectionate carriage of his creature; both which will stake down the heart from vagaries, or giving entertainment to such loose companions as evil thoughts are. Well, then, if we had this heavenly affection strong in us, it would not suffer unwholesome weeds to grow up so near it; either our love would consume those weeds, or those weeds will choke our love.

5. *Exercise faith.*—As the habit of faith is attended with habitual sanctification, so the acts of faith are accompanied with a progress in the degrees of it. That faith which brings Christ to dwell in our souls, will make us often think of our inmate. Faith does realize divine things, and make absent objects as present; and so furnishes fancy with richer streams to bathe itself in than any other principle in the world. As there is a necessity of the use of fancy while the soul is linked to the body, so there is also a necessity of a corrective for it. Reason does in

1 Chyrsostomus.

part regulate it; but it is too weak to do it perfectly, because fancy in most men is stronger than reason: man being the highest of imaginative beings, and the lowest of intelligent, fancy is in its exaltation more than in creatures beneath him, and reason in its detriment more than in creatures above him; and therefore the imagination needs a more skilful guide than reason.[1] Fancy is like fire, "a good servant, but a bad master;" if it march under the conduct of faith, it may be highly serviceable, and, by putting lively colors upon divine truth, may steal away our affections to it. "Faith is the evidence of things not seen," namely, not by a corporeal, but intellectual, eye; and so it will supply the office of sense. It is "the substance of things hoped for;"[2] and if hope be an attendant on faith, our thoughts will surely follow our expectations. The remedy David used, when he was almost stifled with disquieting thoughts, was to excite his soul to a hope and confidence in God: "Why art thou cast down, O my soul? and why art thou disquieted in me? Hope thou in God:"[3] and when they returned upon him, he uses the same diversion.[4] "The peace of God," that is, the reconciliation made by a Mediator between God and us,

---

1 Miranula *De Imaginatione*, cap. 11, 12.

2 Hebrews 11:1.

3 Psalm 42:5.

4 Psalm 42:11.

believingly apprehended, will "keep," or "garrison," our "hearts and minds," or "thoughts," φρουρησει τα νοηματα ὑμων, against all anxious assaults both from within and without.[1] When any vain conceit creeps-up in you, act faith on the intercession of Christ; and consider, "Is Christ thinking of me now in heaven, and pleading for me? and shall I squander away my thoughts on trifles, which will cost me both tears and blushes?" Believingly meditate on the promises; they are a means to cleanse us from the filthiness of the spirit, as well as that of the flesh: "Having therefore these promises, let us cleanse ourselves," etc.[2] If the having them be a motive, the using them will be a means, to attain this end. "Looking at the things which are not seen," preserves us from fainting, and renews the "inward man day by day."[3] These invisible things could not well keep our hearts from fainting, if faith did not first keep the thoughts from wandering from them.

6. *Accustom yourself to a serious meditation every morning.*—Fresh airing our souls in heaven will engender in us purer spirits and nobler thoughts. A morning seasoning would secure us for all the day. Though other necessary thoughts about our callings will and must come in, yet when we have dispatched them, let us attend our morning

1 Philippians 4:6, 7.

2 2 Corinthians 7:1.

3 2 Corinthians 4:16, 18.

theme as our chief companion.[1] As a man that is going with another about some considerable business, (suppose, to Westminster,) though he meets with several friends in the way, and salutes some, and [with] others with whom he has some affairs he spends a little time, yet he quickly returns to his companion, and both together go their intended stage: do thus in the present case. Our minds are active, and will be doing something, though to little purpose; and if they be not fixed upon some noble object, they will, like madmen and fools, be mightily pleased in playing with straws. The thoughts of God were the first visitors David had in the morning; God and his heart met together as soon as he was awake, and kept company all the day after.[2]

In this meditation look both to the *matter* and *manner*.

FIRST. *Look to the matter of your meditation.*—Let it be some truth which will assist you in reviving some languishing grace, or fortify you against some triumphing corruption; for it is our darling sin which does most envenom our thoughts: "As a man thinketh in his heart, so is he."[3] As, if you have a thirst for honor, let your fancy represent the honor of being a child of God and heir of heaven: if

---

1 "That which exists internally forbids the entrance of any thing else from without." *(Nichols' trans.)*

2 Psalm 139:17, 18.

3 Proverbs 23:7.

you are inclined to covetousness, think of the riches stored up in a Saviour, and dispensed by him; if to voluptuousness, fancy the pleasures in the ways of wisdom here, and at God's right hand hereafter. This is to deal with our hearts as Paul with his hearers, to catch them with guile. Stake your soul down to some serious and profitable mystery of religion; as the majesty of God, some particular attribute, his condescension in Christ, the love of our Redeemer, the value of his sufferings, the virtue of his blood, the end of his ascension, the work of the Spirit, the excellency of the soul, beauty of holiness, certainty of death, terror of judgment, torments of hell, and joys of heaven. The heads of the catechism might be taken in order, which would both increase and actuate our knowledge. Why may not that which was the subject of God's innumerable thoughts be the subject of ours?[1] God's thoughts and counsels were concerning Christ, the end of his coming, his death, his precepts of holiness, and promises of life; and that not only speculatively, but with an infinite pleasure in his own glory, and the creature's good, to be accomplished by him. Would it not be work enough for our thoughts all the day, to travel over the length, breadth, height, and depth of the love of Christ? Would the greatness of the journey give us leisure to make any starts out of the way? Having settled the theme for all the day, we shall

1 Psalm 40:5.

find occasional assistances even from worldly businesses; as scholars, who have some exercise to make, find helps in their own course of reading, though the book has no designed respect to their proper theme. Thus, by employing our minds about one thing chiefly, we shall not only hinder them from vain excursions, but make even common objects to be oil to our good thoughts, which otherwise would have been fuel for our bad. Such generous liquor would scent our minds and conversations all the day, [so] that whatsoever motion came into our hearts, would be tinctured with this spirit, and savor of our morning thoughts; as vessels, having been filled with a rich wine, communicate a relish of it to the liquors afterward put into them. We might also more steadily go about our worldly business, if we carry God in our minds; as one foot of the compass will more regularly move about the circumference, when the other remains firm in the center.

Secondly. *Look to the manner of it.*

(1.) *Let it be intent.*—Transitory thoughts are like the glances of the eye—soon on and soon off; they make no clear discovery, and consequently raise no sprightly affections. Let it be one principal subject, and without flitting from it; for if our thoughts be unsteady, we shall find but little warmth; a burning-glass often shifted fires nothing. We must σκοπουντων, "look," "at the things which are not seen," as wistly as men do at a mark they shoot at.[1] Such an intent meditation would "change us into the image," and cast us into the mould, of those truths we think of;[2] it would make our minds more busy about them all the day, as a glaring upon the sun fills our eyes for some time after with the image of it. To this purpose look upon yourselves as deeply concerned in the things you think of. Our minds dwell upon that whereof we apprehend an absolute necessity. A condemned person would scarce think of any thing but procuring a reprieve, and his earnestness for this would bar the door against other intruders.

(2.) *Let it be affectionate and practical.*— Meditation should excite a spiritual delight in God, as it did in the Psalmist: "My meditation of him shall be sweet: I will be glad in the Lord:"[3] and a divine delight would keep-up good thoughts, and keep-out impertinencies. A bare speculation will tire the soul, and, without application and pressing upon the will and affections, will rather chill than warm devotion. It is only by this means that we shall have the efficacy of truth in our wills, and the sweetness in our affections, as well as the motion of it in our understandings. The more operative any truth is in this manner upon us, the less power will other thoughts have to interrupt, and the more

1 2 Corinthians 4:18.

2 2 Corinthians 3:18.

3 Psalm 104:34.

disdainfully will the heart look upon them, if they dare be impudent. Never, therefore, leave thinking of a spiritual subject, till your heart be affected with it. If you think of the evil of sin, leave not till your heart loathe it; if of God, cease not till it mount up in admirations of him. If you think of his mercy, melt for abusing it; if of his sovereignty, awe your heart into obedient resolutions; if of his presence, double your watch over yourself. If you meditate on Christ, make no end till your hearts love him; if of his death, plead the value of it for the justification of your persons, and apply the virtue of it for the sanctification of your natures. Without this practical stamp upon our affections, we shall have light spirits, while we have opportunity to converse with the most serious objects. We often hear foolish thoughts breathing out themselves in a house of mourning, in the midst of coffins and trophies of death, as if men were confident they should never die; whereas none are so ridiculous as to assert they shall live for ever. By this instance in a truth so certainly assented to, we may judge of the necessity of this direction in truths more doubtfully believed.

7. *Draw spiritual inferences from occasional objects.*—David did but wistly "consider the heavens;" and he breaks-out in self-abasement and humble admirations of God.[1] Glean matter of instruction to yourselves, and praise to your Maker, from

1 Psalm 8:3, 4.

every thing you see: it will be a degree of restoration to a state of innocency, since this was Adam's task in Paradise. Dwell not upon any created object only as a virtuoso, to gratify your rational curiosity; but, as a Christian, call religion to the feast, and make a spiritual improvement. No creature can meet our eyes but affords us lessons worthy our thoughts, beside the general notices of the power and wisdom of the Creator. Thus may the sheep read us a lecture of patience, the dove of innocence, the ant and bee raise blushes in us for our sluggishness, and the stupid ox and dull ass correct and shame our ungrateful ignorance.[1] And since our Saviour did set-forth his own excellency in a sensible dress, the consideration of those metaphors by an acute fancy would garnish-out divine truths more deliciously, and conduct us into a more inward knowledge of the mysteries of the gospel. He whose eyes are open cannot want an instructor, unless he wants a heart. Thus may a tradesman spiritualize the matter he works upon, and make his commodities serve in wholesome meditations to his mind, and at once enrich both his soul and his coffers; yea, and in part restore the creatures to the happiness of answering a great end of their creation, which man deprived them of, when he subjected them to vanity. Such a view of spiritual truths in sensible pictures would clear our knowledge, purify our fancies, animate

1 Isaiah 1:3.

our affections, encourage our graces, disgrace our vices, and both argue and shame us into duty; and thus take away all the causes of our wild, wandering thoughts at once. And a frequent exercise of this method would beget and support a habit of thinking well, and weaken, if not expel, a habit of thinking ill.

II. The second sort of directions are *for the preventing [of] bad thoughts.* And to this purpose,

1. *Exercise frequent humiliations.*—Pride exposes us to impatient and disquieting thoughts; whereas humility clears-up a calm and serenity in the soul. It is Agur's advice, to be humbled particularly for evil thoughts.[1] Frequent humiliations will dead the fire within, and make the sparks the fewer. The deeper the plough sinks, the more the weeds are killed, and the ground fitted for good grain. Men do not easily fall into those sins for which they have been deeply humbled. Vain conceits love to reside most in jolly hearts; but "by the sadness of the countenance the heart is made better."[2] There is more of wisdom, or wise consideration, in a composed and graciously mournful spirit; whereas carnal mirth and sports cause the heart to evaporate into lightness and folly. The more we are humbled for them, the more our hatred of them will be fomented, and, consequently, the more prepared shall we be to give

1 Proverbs 30:32.

2 Ecclesiastes 7:3, 4.

them a repulse upon any bold intrusion.

2. *Avoid entangling yourselves with the world.*—This clay will clog our minds, and "a dirty happiness" will engender but dirty thoughts.[1] Who were so foolish to have "inward thoughts that their houses should continue for ever," but those "that trusted in their riches?"[2] If the world possess our souls, it will breed carking thoughts: much business meets with crosses, and then it breeds murmuring thoughts; and sometimes it is crowned with success, and then it starts proud and self-applauding thoughts. "They that will be rich fall into many foolish and hurtful lusts;"[3] such lusts that make men fools; and one part of folly is to have wild and senseless fancies. Mists and fogs are in the lower region near the earth, but reach not that next the heavens. Were we free from earthly affections, these gross vapors could not so easily disturb our minds; but if the world once settle in our hearts, we shall never want the fumes of it to fill our heads. And as covetous desires will stuff us with foolish imaginations, so they will smother any good thought cast into us; as "the thorns" of worldly cares "choked" the good seed, and made it "unfruitful."[4] As we are to rejoice in the world as though we rejoiced not, so,

1 Augustinus *De Civitate Dei,* lib. x.

2 Psalm 49:6, 11.

3 1 Timothy 6:9.

4 Matthew 13:22.

by the same reason, we should think of the world as though we thought not. A conformity with the world in affection is inconsistent with a change of the frame of the mind.[1]

3. *Avoid idleness.*—Serious callings do naturally compose men's spirits; but too much recreation makes them blaze-out in vanity. Idle souls, as well as idle persons, will be ranging. As idleness in a state is both the mother and nurse of faction, and in the natural body gives birth and increase to many diseases by enfeebling the natural heat; so it both kindles and foments many light and unprofitable imaginations in the soul, which would be sufficiently diverted, if the active mind were kept intent upon some stated work. So truly may that which was said of the servant, be applied to our nobler part, that it will be "wicked," if once it degenerates into "slothfulness" in its proper charge. ("Thou wicked and slothful servant."[2]) As empty minds are the fittest subjects for extravagant fooleries, so vacant times are the fittest seasons. While we sleep, the importunate "enemy" within, as well as the envious adversary without us, will have a successful opportunity to "sow the tares:"[3] whereas a constant employment frustrates the attempt, and discourages the devil, because he sees we are not at leisure.

1 Romans 12:2.

2 Matthew 25:26.

3 Matthew 13:25.

Therefore, when any sinful motion steps-in, double your vigor about your present business, and the foolish impertinent will sneak out of thy heart at this discountenance. So true is that in this case which Pharaoh falsely imagined in another, that the more we "labor," the less we shall "regard vain words."[1] As Satan is prevented by diligence in our callings, so sometimes the Spirit visits us, and fills us with holy affections, at such seasons; as Christ appeared to Peter and other disciples, when they were a-fishing;[2] and usually manifested his grace to men, when they were engaged in their useful businesses, or religious services. But these motions, as we may observe by the way, which come from the Spirit, are not to put us out of our way, but to assist us in our walking in it, and further us both in our attendance on, and success in, our duties. To this end, look upon the work of your callings as the work of God, which ought to be done in obedience to Him, as he has set you to be useful in the community. Thus a holy exercise of our callings would sanctify our minds, and, by prepossessing them with solid business, we should leave little room for any spider to weave its cobwebs.

4. *Awe your hearts with the thoughts of God's omniscience, especially the discovery of it at the last judgment.*—We are very much atheists in the

1 Exodus 5:9.

2 John 21:3, 4.

concern of this attribute; for though it be notionally believed, yet for the most part it is practically denied. God "understands" all our "thoughts afar off;"[1] as he knew every creature which lay hid in the chaos and undigested lump of matter. God is in us all;[2] as much in us all, as he is above us all; yea, in every creek and chink and point of our hearts. Not an atom in the spirits of all men in the world, but is obvious to that all-seeing eye, which knows every one of those things that come into our minds.[3] God knows both the order and confusion of them, and can better tell their natures one by one than Adam named the creatures. Fancy, then, that you hear the sound of the last trumpet; that you see God's tribunal set, and his omniscience calling-out singly all the secrets of your heart. Would not the consideration of this allay the heat of all other imaginations? If a foolish thought break-in, consider, "What, if God, who knows this, should presently call me to judgment for this sinful glance?" Say, with the church, "Shall not God search this out?"[4] Is it fit either for God's glory or our interest, that when he comes to make inquisition in us, he should find such a nasty dunghill, and swarms of Egyptian lice and frogs creeping up and down our chambers? Were our heads and hearts possessed by

1 Psalm 139:2.

2 Ephesians 4:6.

3 Ezekiel 11:5.

4 Psalm 44:21.

this substantial truth, we should be ashamed to think what we shall be ashamed to own at the last day.

5. *Keep a constant watch over your hearts.*—David desires God to "set a watch before the door of his lips;"[1] much more should we desire, that God would keep the door of our hearts. We should have grace stand sentinel there especially: for words have an outward bridle; they may disgrace a man, and impair his interest and credit; but thoughts are unknown, if undiscovered by words. If a man knew what time the thief would come to rob him, he would watch. We know, we have thieves within us to steal away our hearts; therefore, when they are so near us, we should watch against a surprise; and the more carefully, because they are so extraordinarily sudden in their rise, and quick in their motion. Our minds are like idle school-boys, that will be frisking from one place to another, if the master's back be turned, and playing instead of learning. Let a strict hand be kept over our affections, those "wild beasts within us,"[2] because they many times force the understanding to pass a judgment according to their pleasure, not its own sentiment. Young men should be most intent upon their guard, because their fancies gather vigor from their youthful heat, which fires a world of squibs in a day; (which madmen, and those which have hot diseases, are subject

1 Psalm 141:3.

2 Plato.

to, because of the excessive inflammation of their brains) and partly because they are not sprung-up to a maturity of knowledge, which would breed and foster better thoughts, and discover the plausible pretences of vain affections. There are particular seasons when we must double our guard; as when incentives are present, that may set some inward corruption on a flame. Timothy's office was to exhort younger, as well as elder, women; and the apostle wishes him to do it "with all purity," or "chastity," εν πασῃ αγνειᾳ,[1] that a temptation, lying in ambush for him, might not take his thoughts and affections unguarded. Engage your diligence more at solitary times and in the night, wherein freedom from business gives an opportunity to an unsanctified imagination to conjure up a thousand evil spirits; whence perhaps it is that the Psalmist tells us, God had "tried him in the night," and found him holy.[2] The solitary cave tainted Lot with incest, who had preserved himself fresh in the midst of the salt lusts of Sodom.[3, 4] In ill company, wherein we may be occasionally cast, there is need of an exacter observation of our hearts: lest corrupt steams, which rise from them

1 1 Timothy 5:2.

2 Psalm 17:3.

3 "The little chamber of my thoughts kept my fears in constant exercise."—HIERONYMUS. *(Nichols' trans.)*

4 Genesis 19:30.

as vapors from lakes and minerals, being breathed-in by us, may tincture our spirits, or as those μιασματα, ["distempered particles,"] which, as physicians tell us, exhaling from consumptive persons, do by inspiration steal into our blood, and convey a contagion to us. And though "above all keepings" and watchings we are to keep and watch our hearts, because "out of them are the issues of life;"[1] yet we must walk the rounds about our senses and members of the body, as the wise man there advises: *the mouth*, which utters wickedness;[2] *the eyes*, which are brokers to make bargains for the heart;[3] and *the feet*, which are agents to run on the errands of sin.[4] And the rather must we watch over our senses, because we are naturally more ready to follow the motions of them, as having had a longer acquaintance and familiarity with them before we grew up to the use of reason. Besides, most of our thoughts creep-in first at the windows of sense:[5] the eye and the ear robbed Eve of original righteousness; and the eye rifled David both of his justice and chastity.[6] If the "eyes behold strange

1 Proverbs 4:23.

2 Proverbs 4:24.

3 Proverbs 4:25.

4 Proverbs 4:26.

5 Plotinus describes thought thus: "The resemblance and community which exists between outward things and those which are within."—*Ennead.* lib. i. *(Nichols' trans.)*

6 "The heart and the eyes are the negotiating agents of sin." *(Nichols' trans.)*

women," the "heart will utter perverse things;"[1] perverse thoughts will sparkle from a rolling eye. Revelrout is usual where there is a negligent government. "He that hath no rule over his own spirit, is like a city that is broken down, and without walls,"[2] where any thieves may go in and out at pleasure.

III. The third sort of directions are *for the ordering of evil thoughts*, when they do intrude. And,

1. *Examine them.*—Look often into your heart to see what it is doing; and what thoughts you find dabbling in it, call to an account: inquire what business they have, what their errand and design is, whence they come, and whither they tend. David asked his soul the reason of its troubled thoughts: "Why art thou disquieted, O my soul?"[3] so ask your heart the reason why it entertains such ill company, and by what authority they come there; and leave not chiding, till you have put it to the blush. Bring every thought to the test of the Word. Asaph had envious thoughts at "the prosperity of the wicked,"[4] which had almost tripped him up, and laid him on his back. And these had blown-up atheistical thoughts, that God did not much regard whether his commands were kept or no; as though God had untied the link between duty and reward, and the

---

1 Proverbs 23:33.

2 Proverbs 25:28.

3 Psalm 42:11.

4 Psalm 73:2, 3.

breach of his laws were the readiest means to a favorable recompense. "I have cleansed my heart in vain."[1] But when he weighed things in the balance of the sanctuary, by the holy rules of God's patience and justice,[2] he sees the brutishness of his former conceits. "So foolish was I, and ignorant: I was as a beast before thee;"[3] and, he makes an improvement of them, to excite his desire for God, and delight in him.[4] Let us compare our thoughts with Scripture rules. "Comparing spiritual things with spiritual," is the way to understand them; comparing spiritual sins with spiritual commands, is the way to know them; and comparing spiritual vices with spiritual graces, is the way to loathe them. Take not, then, any thing upon trust from a crazy fancy; nor, without a scrutiny, believe that faculty whereby dogs dream, and animals perform their natural exploits.

2. *Check them at the first appearance.*—If they bear upon them a palpable mark of sin, bestow not upon them the honor of an examination. If the leprosy appear in their foreheads, thrust them, as the priests did Uzziah, out of the temple; or as David answered his wicked solicitors: "Depart from me, ye evil-doers: for I will keep the commandments of my God."[5] Though we cannot hinder them from

1 Psalm 73:13.

2 Psalm 73:17.

3 Psalm 73:22.

4 Psalm 73:25.

5 Psalm 119:115.

haunting us, yet we may from lodging in us. The very sparkling of an abominable motion in our hearts is as little to be looked upon, as the color of wine in a glass by a man inclined to drunkenness. Quench them instantly, as you would do a spark of fire in a heap of straw. We must not treat with them: Paul's resolve is a good pattern—not to "confer with flesh and blood."[1,2] We do not debate whether we should shake a viper off our hands. If it be plainly a sinful motion, a treaty with it is a degree of disobedience; for a putting it to the question, whether we should suckle it, is to question whether God should be obeyed or no. If it "savor not the things of God," hear not its reasons, and compliment it with no less indignation than our Saviour did his officious disciple upon his carnal advice: "Get thee behind me, Satan."[3] Excuse it not, because it is little. Small vapors may compact themselves into great clouds, and obstruct our sight of heaven; a little poison may spread its venom through a great quantity of meat. We know not how big a small motion, like a crocodile's egg, may grow, and how ravenous the breed may prove: it

---

1 "This Hannibal must be overcome by valor, and not by delay." An allusion to the retarding stratagems by which Fabius warded-off the destruction impending over Rome from the hands of the consummate general of Carthage, and by which he immortalized himself as "the Delayer." *(Nicohls' trans.)*

2 Galatians 1:16.

3 Matthew 16:22, 23.

may, if entertained, force our judgment, drag our will, and make all our affections bedlams.[1] Besides, since the fancy is that power in us upon which the devil can immediately imprint his suggestions, and that we know not what army he has to back any sinful motion if once the gate be set open, let us crush the brat betimes, and fling the head over the wall, to discourage the party. Well, then, let us be ashamed to cherish that in our thoughts which we should be ashamed should break-out in our words or actions. Therefore, as soon as you perceive it base, spit it out with detestation, as you do a thing you unexpectedly find ungrateful to your palate.

3. *Improve them.*—Poisons may be made medicinable. Let the thoughts of old sins stir-up a commotion of anger and hatred. We feel shiverings in our spirits and a motion in our blood at the very thought of a bitter potion we have formerly taken: why may we not do that spiritually which the very frame and constitution of our bodies does naturally, upon the calling a loathsome thing to mind? The Romans' sins were transient; but the shame was renewed every time they reflected on them: ("Whereof ye are now ashamed"[2]) they reacted a

1 "By this is my weakness shown, that abominable fancies rush into my mind much more easily than they are expelled."—Kempis *De Imitatione Christi*, lib. iii., cap. 20. *(Nicohls' trans.)*

2 Romans 6:21.

detestation instead of the pleasure; so should the revivings of old sins in our memories be entertained with our sighs, rather than our joy. We should also manage the opportunity so as to promote some further degrees of our conversion: "I thought on my ways, and turned my feet unto thy testimonies."[1] There is not the most hellish motion, but we may strike some sparks from it, to kindle our love to God, renew our repentance, raise our thankfulness, or quicken our obedience. Is it a blasphemous motion against God? It gives you a just occasion thence to awe your heart into a deeper reverence of his majesty. Is it a lustful thought? Open the flood-gates of your godly sorrow, and groan for your original sin. Is it a remembrance of your former sin? Let it wind-up your heart in the praises of Him who delivered you from it. Is it to tempt you from duty? Endeavor to be more zealous in the performance of it. Is it to set you at a distance from God? Resolve to be a light shining the clearer in that darkness, and let it excite you to a closer adherence to him. Are they envious thoughts which steal upon you? Let thankfulness be the product, that you enjoy so much as you do, and more than you deserve. Let Satan's fiery darts inflame your love rather than your lust; and, like a skillful pilot, make use of the violence of the winds and raging of the sea to further you in your spiritual voyage. This is to beat the devil and our own hearts

1 Psalm 119:59.

with their own weapons, who will have little stomach to fight with those arms wherewith they see themselves wounded. There is not a remembrance of the worst objects but may be improved to humility and thankfulness; as St. Paul never thought of his old persecuting, but he sank-down in humiliation, and mounted-up in admirations of the riches of grace.

4. *Continue your resistance, if they still importune thee, and lay not down your weapons till they wholly shrink from thee.*—As the wise man speaks of a fool's words, so I may, not only of our blacker, but our more aërial, fancies: "The beginning of" them "is foolishness;" but if suffered to gather strength, they may end in "mischievous madness."[1] Therefore, if they do continue or re-assume their arms, we must continue and re-assume our shield: "Above all, taking the shield of faith." (Αναλαϐοντες, "Taking up again."[2]) Resistance makes the devil and his imps fly; but forbearance makes them impudent. In a battle, when one party faints and retreats, it adds new spirits to the enemy, that was almost broken before: so will these motions be the more vigorous, if they perceive we begin to flag. That encouraging command, "Resist the devil, and he will flee from you,"[3] implies not only the

1 Ecclesiastes 10:13.

2 Ephesians 6:16.

3 James 4:7.

beginning a fight, but continuance in it till he does fly. We must not leave the field, till they cease their importunity; nor increase their courage by our own cowardice.

5. *Join supplication with your opposition.*—"Watch and pray," are sometimes linked together.[1] The diligence and multitude of our enemies should urge us to watch, that we be not surprised; and our own weakness and proneness to presumption should make us pray, that we may be powerfully assisted. Be as frequent in soliciting God as they are in soliciting you; as they knock at your heart for entrance, so do you knock at heaven for assistance. And take this for your comfort: as the devil takes their parts, so Christ will take yours at his Father's throne; he that prayed that the devil might not winnow Peter's faith, will intercede that your own heart may not winnow yours. If the waves come upon you, and you are ready to sink, cry out, with Peter, "Master, I perish;" and you shall feel his hand raising you, and the winds and waves rebuked into obedience by him. The very motion of your hearts heavenward at such a time is a refusal of the thought that presses upon you, and will be so put upon your account. When any of these buzzing flies discompose you, or more violent hurricanes shake your minds, cry out, with David, "Unite my heart to fear thy name"[2] and a powerful

1 Matthew 26:41.

2 Psalm 86:11, 12.

word will soon silence these disturbing enemies, and settle your souls in a calm and a praising posture.

IV. A fourth sort of directions is *concerning good motions;* whether they spring naturally from a gracious principle, or are peculiarly breathed in by the Spirit. There are ordinary bubblings of grace in a renewed mind, as there are of sins in an unregenerate heart; for grace is as active a principle as any, because it is a participation of the divine nature. But there are other thoughts darted-in beyond the ordinary strain of thinking; which, like the beams of the sun, evidence both themselves and their original. And, as concerning these motions joined together, take these directions in short:—

1. *Welcome and entertain them.*—As it is our happiness, as well as our duty, to stifle evil motions, so it is our misery, as well as our sin, to extinguish heavenly. Strange fire should be presently quenched; but that which descends from heaven upon the altar of a holy soul, must be kept alive by quickening meditation.[1] When a holy thought lights suddenly upon you which has no connection with any antecedent business in your mind, provided it be not unseasonable, nor hinder you from any absolutely necessary duty either of religion or your calling, receive it as a messenger from heaven, and the rather because it is a stranger. You know not but you may

1 Polycarp, *in Epist. ad Philip.*, terms holy persons ["the altars of God"].

entertain an angel, yea, something greater than an angel, even the Holy Ghost. Open all the powers of your souls, like so many organ-pipes, to receive the breath of this Spirit when he blows upon you. It is a sign of an agreeableness between the heart and heaven, when we close-with and preserve spiritual motions. We need not stand long to examine them: they are evident by their holiness, sweetness, and spirituality. We may as easily discern them, as we can exotic plants from those that grow naturally in our own soil, or as a palate at the first taste can distinguish between a rich and generous wine and a rough water. The thoughts instilled by the Spirit of adoption are not violent, tumultuous, full of perturbation; but, like himself, "gentle" and dove-like solicitings, warm and holy impulses, and, when cherished, leave the soul in a more humble, heavenly, pure, and believing temper than they found it.[1] It is a high aggravation of sin to "resist the Holy Ghost."[2] Yet we may quench his motions by neglect as well as by opposition, and by that means lose both the profit and pleasure which would have attended the entertainment. Salvation came both to Zacchaeus's house and heart, upon embracing the first motion [which] our Saviour was pleased to make [to] him. Had he slighted *that*, it is uncertain whether another should have been bestowed

1 Galatians 5:22.

2 Acts 7:51.

upon him. The more such sprouts are planted and nourished in us, the less room will stinking weeds have to root themselves, and disperse their influence. And for your own good thoughts, feed them, and keep them alive, that they may not be like a blaze of straw, which takes birth and expires the same minute. Brood upon them, and kill them not, as some birds do their young ones by too often flying from their nests. David kept-up a staple of sound and good thoughts: he would scarce else have desired God to "try and know" them, had they been only some few weak flashes at uncertain times: "Try me, and know my thoughts."[1]

2. *Improve them for those ends to which they naturally tend.*—It is not enough to give them a bare reception, and forbear the smothering of them, but we must consider what affections are proper to be raised by them, either in the search of some truth, or performance of some duty. Those gleams which shoot into us on the sudden have some lesson sealed up in them, to be opened and learned by us. When Peter, upon the crowing of the cock, called to mind his Master's admonition, "he thought thereon," and "wept:"[2] he did not only receive the spark, but kindled a suitable affection. A choice graft, though kept very carefully by us, yet if not presently set, will wither, and disappoint our expectation of the

1 Psalm 139:23.

2 Mark 14:72.

desired fruit. No man is without some secret whispers to dissuade him from some alluring and busy sin:—"God speaketh once, yea twice, that he may withdraw man from his purpose"[1]—as Cain had by an audible voice,[2] which had he observed to the damping the revengeful motion against his brother, he had prevented his brother's death, his own despair and eternal ruin. Have you any motion to seek God's face, as David had? Let your hearts reply, "Thy face, Lord, will I seek."[3] The address will be most acceptable at such a time, when your heart is tuned by One that "searcheth the deep things of God,"[4] and knows his mind, and what airs are most delightful to Him. Let our motion be quick in any duty which the Spirit does suggest; and while he heaves our hearts, and oils our wheels, we shall do more in any religious service, and that more pleasantly and successfully, than at another time with all our own art and industry; for his injections are like water poured into a pump to raise-up more; and as Satan's motions are not without a main body to second them, so neither do the Spirit's go unattended, without a sufficient strength to assist the entertainers of them. Well, then, lie not at anchor, when a fresh gale would fill thy sails; but lay hold of the

1 Job 33:14, 17.

2 Genesis 4:7.

3 Psalm 27:8.

4 1 Corinthians 2:10.

present opportunity. These seasons are often like those influences from certain conjunctions of the planets, which, if not (according to the astrologer's opinion) presently applied, pass away, and return not again in many ages: so the Spirit's breathings are often so determined, that if they be not entertained with suitable affections, the time will be unregainable, and the same gracious opportunities of a sweet intercourse may be for ever lost; for God will not have his Holy Spirit dishonored in "always striving" with willful man.[1] When Judas neglected our Saviour's advertisement,[2] the devil quickly enters, and hurries him to the execution of his traitorous project,[3] and he never meets with any motion afterwards, but from his new master, and that eternally fatal both to his body and soul.

3. *Refer them, if possible, to assist your morning-meditation.*—That, like little brooks arising from several springs, they may meet in one channel, and compose a more useful stream. What straggling good thoughts arise, though they may owe their birth to several occasions, and tend divers ways, yet list them in the service of that truth to which you have committed the government of your mind that day: as constables, in a time of necessary business for the king, take-up men that are going about their

1 Genesis 6:3.

2 John 13:21.

3 John 13:27.

honest and lawful occasions, and force them to join in one employ for the public service. Many accidental glances, as was observed before, will serve both to fix and illustrate your morning-proposition. But if it be an extraordinary injection, and cannot be referred to your standing thesis, follow it, and let your thoughts run whither it will lead you: a theme of the Spirit's setting is better than one of our own choosing.

4. *Record the choicer of them.*—We may have occasion to look back upon them another time, either as grounds of comfort in some hour of temptation, or directions in some sudden emergency, but constantly as persuasive engagements to our necessary duty. Thus they may lie by us for further use, as money in our purse. Since "Mary kept and pondered" the short sayings of our Saviour "in her heart,"[1] συμϐαλλουσα, "committing and fitting" them, as it were, in her common place book,[2] why should not we also preserve the whispers of that Spirit, who receives from the same mouth and hand what he both speaks and shows to us?[3] It is pity the dust and filings of choicer metals, which may one time be melted-down into a mass, should be lost in a heap of drossy thoughts. If we do not remember them, but, like children, are taken with their novelty

1 Luke 2:19, 51.

2 "The Greek verb here used signifies, 'to fit together.'" —Hesychius. *(Nichols' trans.)*

3 John 16:13, 14.

more than their substance, and, like John Baptist's hearers, rejoice in their light only "for a season,"[1] it will discourage the Spirit from sending any more; and then our hearts will be empty; and we know who stands ready to clap-in his hellish swarms and legions. But, howsoever we do, God will record our good thoughts as our excusers, if we improve them; as our accusers, if we reject them: and as he took notice how often he had appeared to Solomon,[2] so he will take notice how often his Spirit has appeared to us, and write-down every motion whereby we have been solicited, that they may be witnesses of his endeavors for our good, and our own wilfulness.

5. *Back them with ejaculations.*—Let our hearts be ready to attend every injection from heaven with a motion to it, since it is ingratitude to receive a present without returning an acknowledgment to the benefactor. As God turns his thoughts of us into promises, so let us turn our thoughts of him into prayers; and since his regards of us are darted in beams upon us, let them be reflected back upon him in thankfulness for the gift, and earnestness both for the continuance and increase of such impressions; as David prayed that God would not take his Holy Spirit from him who had inspired him with his penitential resolutions.[3] To what purpose does the Holy

1 John 5:35.
2 1 Kings 11:9.
3 Psalm 51:11.

Ghost descend upon us, but to declare to us "the things that are freely given to us of God?"[1] And is it fit for us to hear such a declaration without a quick suitable reflection? Since the Comforter is to bring to our remembrance what Christ both spoke and did,[2] it must be for the same end for which they were both spoken and acted by him—which was, to bring us to a near converse with God. Therefore, when the Spirit renews in our minds a gospel-truth, let us turn it into a present plea, and be God's remembrancers of his own promises, as the Spirit is our remembrancer of divine truths. We need not doubt some rich fruit of the application at such a season, since, without question, the impressions [which] the Spirit stamps upon us are as much "according to God's will" as the intercessions he makes for us.[3] Therefore, when any holy thought does advance itself in our souls, the most grateful reception we can bestow upon it will be to suffer our hearts to be immediately fired by it, and imitate with a glowing devotion the royal prophet, in that form he has drawn-up to our hands: "O Lord God of Abraham, Isaac, and of Israel, our fathers, keep this for ever in the imagination of the thoughts of the heart of thy servant, and prepare my heart unto thee."[4] This will

1 1 Corinthians 2:12.

2 John 14:26.

3 Romans 8:27.

4 1 Chronicles 29:18.

be an encouragement to God to send more such guests into our hearts; and by an affectionate entertainment of them, we shall gain both a habit of thinking well, and a stock too.

NOTES

NOTES

.ı I accountable to God?
:ach of us will give an account of himself to God. Romans 14:12 (NIV).

Has God seen all my ways?
Everything is uncovered and laid bare before the eyes of him to whom we must give account. Hebrews 4:13 (NIV).

Does he charge me with sin?
But the Scripture declares that the whole world is a prisoner of sin. Galatians 3:22 (NIV).
All have sinned and fall short of the glory of God. Romans 3:23 (NIV).

Will he punish sin?
The soul who sins is the one who will die. Ezekiel 18:4 (NIV).
For the wages of sin is death, but the gift of God is eternal life in Christ Jesus our Lord. Romans 6:23 (NIV).

Must I perish?
He is patient with you, not wanting anyone to perish, but everyone to come to repentance. 2 Peter 3:9 (NIV).

How can I escape?
Believe in the Lord Jesus, and you will be saved. Acts 16:31 (NIV).

Is he able to save me?
Therefore he is able to save completely those who come to God through him. Hebrews 7:25 (NIV).

Is he willing?
Christ Jesus came into the world to save sinners. 1 Timothy 1:15 (NIV).

Am I saved on believing?
Whoever believes in the Son has eternal life, but whoever rejects the Son will not see life, for God's wrath remains on him. John 3:36 (NIV).

Can I be saved now?
Now is the time of God's favor, now is the day of salvation. 2 Corinthians 6:2 (NIV).

As I am?
Whoever comes to me I will never drive away. John 6:37 (NIV).

Shall I not fall away?
Him who is able to keep you from falling. Jude 1:24 (NIV).

If saved, how should I live?
Those who live should no longer live for themselves but for him who died for them and was raised again. 2 Corinthians 5:15 (NIV).

What about death and eternity?
I am going there to prepare a place for you. I will come back and take you to be with me that you also may be where I am. John 14:2-3 (NIV).

Made in the USA
Middletown, DE
02 August 2019